SURVIVING R

Other How To Books on jobs and careers

Finding a Job in Computers
How to Apply for a Job
How to Be a Freelance Journalist
How to Be a Freelance Sales Agent
How to Be a Freelance Secretary
How to Become an Au Pair
How to Do Voluntary Work Abroad
How to Find Temporary Work Abroad
How to Get a Job Abroad
How to Get a Job in Hotels & Catering
How to Get a Job in America
How to Get a Job in Australia
How to Get a Job in Europe
How to Get a Job in France
How to Get a Job in Germany
How to Get a Job in Travel & Tourism
How to Know Your Rights at Work

How to Manage Your Career
How to Market Yourself
How to Return to Work
How to Start a New Career
How to Work from Home
How to Work in an Office
How to Work in Retail
How to Work with Dogs
How to Work with Horses
How to Write a CV That Works
Living & Working in China
Surviving Redundancy
Working as a Holiday Rep
Working in Japan
Working on Contract Worldwide
Working on Cruise Ships

Other titles in preparation

The How to Series now contains more than 150 titles in the following categories:

Business Matters
Family Reference
Jobs & Careers
Living & Working Abroad
Student Handbooks
Successful Writing

Please send for a free copy of the latest catalogue for full details
(see back cover for address).

JOBS & CAREERS

SURVIVING REDUNDANCY

How to take charge of yourself
and your future

Laurel Alexander

How To Books

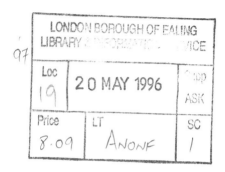

Cartoons by Mike Flanagan

British Library Cataloguing-in-publication data
A catalogue record for this book is available from the British Library.

Copyright © 1996 by Laurel Alexander.

First published in 1996 by How To Books Ltd, Plymbridge House, Estover Road, Plymouth PL6 7PZ, United Kingdom.

All rights reserved. No part of this work may be reproduced or stored in an information retrieval system (other than short extracts for purposes of review), without the express permission of the Publishers in writing.

Note: The material contained in this book is set out in good faith for general guidance and no liability can be accepted for loss or expense incurred as a result of relying in particular circumstances on statements made in the book. The laws and regulations are complex and liable to change, and readers should check the current position with the relevant authorities before making personal arrangements.

Produced for How To Books by Deer Park Productions.

Typeset by Concept Communications (Design & Print) Ltd, Crayford, Kent.
Printed and bound by The Cromwell Press, Broughton Gifford, Melksham, Wiltshire.

Contents

	List of illustrations	8
	Preface	9
1	**Coping with the first few weeks**	11
	Reacting to the redundancy	11
	Saying goodbye	13
	Dealing with loss	14
	Coping with the first few days	21
	Checklist for the first few weeks	24
	Case studies	25
	Discussion points	26
2	**Handling your finances**	27
	Organising your finances	27
	Your low cost or no cost lifestyle	31
	Defining your needs and wants	32
	Redefining your material values	33
	Case studies	35
	Discussion points	35
3	**Making changes**	36
	Coping with change	36
	Looking after your health	38
	Using positive thinking	42
	Managing your time	43
	Case studies	47
	Discussion points	48
4	**Re-defining your value system**	49
	Why work?	49
	Assessing your skills	53
	Your ideal career	56
	Case studies	58
	Discussion points	59

5	**Setting up a career development strategy**	60
	Researching the job market	60
	Returning to study	62
	Organising your jobsearch strategy	62
	Making speculative contacts	66
	Using the media	66
	Starting to network	68
	Creating your own job	72
	Case studies	72
	Discussion points	73
6	**Overcoming barriers**	74
	What are barriers?	74
	Building up shattered confidence	80
	Breaking down expectations	82
	Looking at our values	82
	Case studies	83
	Discussion points	84
7	**Choosing a mode of work**	85
	Choosing interim management	85
	Choosing term-time working	85
	Choosing to work from home	86
	Buying a franchise	86
	Being a portfolio person	86
	Choosing temporary work	86
	Choosing flexi-time	87
	Choosing to jobshare	87
	Choosing contract work	87
	Choosing part-time work	87
	Choosing to work abroad	88
	Choosing to be self employed	88
	Case studies	93
	Discussion points	95
8	**Selling yourself**	96
	Communicating in different ways	96
	Creating your image and style	99
	Reading the job advertisement	101
	Using the telephone	102
	Creating your CV	103
	Effective letter writing	105
	Filling in application forms	109
	Attending an interview	109
	Case studies	115
	Discussion points	115

9	**Training and education**	116
	What is learning?	116
	Basic education	120
	Further education	121
	Adult education	121
	Access courses	121
	Higher education	122
	Open and distance learning	122
	Government schemes	122
	How to find out about courses	122
	Qualifications	123
	Costs and funding	124
	Case studies	126
	Discussion points	127
10	**Your way forward**	128
	Using what you have	128
	Letting go of being a victim	129
	Taking responsibility	130
	Using effective thinking skills	131
	Giving yourself positive strokes	133
	Ten steps to feeling positive	134
	Improving your self image	134
	Developing a philosophical attitude	135
	Your positive achievements journal	136
	Setting and achieving goals	136
	Endings and beginnings	137
	Case studies	137
	Discussion points	138

Glossary	142
Useful addresses	148
Further reading	151
Index	155

List of Illustrations

1.	The grieving cycle	17
2.	Benefit leaflet guide	28
3.	Your budget plan	30
4.	Looking after yourself	37
5.	Signs of stress	39
6.	Your time management diary	46
7.	The bridge of life	50
8.	Know thyself and get a better job	57
9.	Recording your agency contacts	65
10.	Recording your company contacts	66
11.	Using the media	69
12.	Your business skills assessment	90
13.	A chronological CV model	106
14.	A speculative letter	110
15.	A letter of application	111
16.	A specimen application form	112
17.	Your goals record	139
18.	Your action plan	141

Preface

Redundancy can be viewed as an opportunity for positive change. You could use this time for self discovery and use the information to re-focus your work needs and career direction. Most of us don't like to have change forced upon us, but when it happens, we have a choice: to give in, believing that we are a victim of fate, or to believe in ourselves, our experiences, skills and knowledge and move forward with anticipation and pride.

Career development is not only about the facts of skills analysis, job-search strategies and information giving. It is about who you are, what makes you tick, your needs and wants, your dreams and hopes. If you base your career plan on who you are rather than what you think you should be doing, you are far more likely to choose the right career path that offers you personal growth and material fulfilment.

This book is designed to lead you over the stepping stones of surviving redundancy. But it is more than that. It is about self-knowledge — the foundation to your new career. Your route will take you through:

- coping with the first few weeks
- organising your finances
- making changes
- looking after your health
- using positive thinking
- managing your time
- organising your jobsearch strategy
- starting to network
- building up confidence
- choosing a mode of work
- selling yourself
- training and education
- developing a philosophical attitude
- setting and achieving goals.

Finally, I would like to acknowledge the help of: my husband Michael for his encouragement, and Angie Dickson for her professional advice.

Laurel Alexander

IS THIS YOU?

Redundant   Unemployed

                Looking for work

Wanting a new career   Career counsellor

              Working in personnel

Worried about your job   Looking for a career path

       Needing to take charge of your career

Ready for a challenge   Looking for advice on training

         Thinking about self employment

Ready to re-evaluate your life   Seeking new horizons

                 Careers officer

Employment consultant   Citizens advice worker

            Considering cutting staff

Redundancy counsellor   Trainer

          Fed up with your current job

Returning to work   Working for Employment Services

              Available for work

Outplacement consultant   Counsellor

            Looking for motivation

Ready for a change   Wanting to re-train

       Needing reassurance after a job loss

Seeking career strategy   Seeking to re-invent yourself

      Wanting to identify your work skills

        Seeking new ways of working

1
Coping with the First Few Weeks

REACTING TO THE REDUNDANCY

'I'm sorry to have to tell you . . .'. There is no good way of being told that your job is no longer there for you to have!

You may hear rumours for months before anything concrete happens. You may see other people go over a period of time. The company may become less busy. You wonder and worry.

During this time you may feel hopeful, frustrated and anxious. You may feel inclined to try even harder so that you won't be the one to go. Then, when the inevitable happens — you will feel stunned. You might go through a period of denial — a time when it doesn't sink in, you might have feelings of euphoria without the implications being acknowledged. You may experience elation at the thought of release from a job you hated. You may feel threatened over losing financial security. You may feel sad at the idea of losing touch with friends.

When it comes out of the blue, it is a huge shock and there is more likelihood of a grudge against the company. Why didn't they let anyone know?

Redundancy is now becoming an accepted word in our society. The structure of work is changing. Once we followed the traditional pattern of:

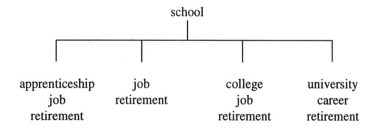

Now we have:

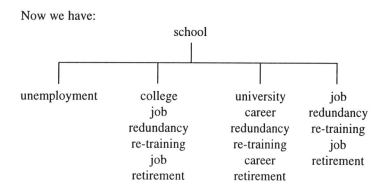

Redundancy is not necessarily linked to talent — it is usually about cost effectiveness and the restructuring of the business. But it may not feel like that when it happens to you.

We spend a lot of our waking hours at work. We gain the skills and knowledge for the job, we apply for the position, attend an interview and we then put time and effort into actually working.

Why do we work?

There are several reasons why we work — the main ones being power, status and money. We need to put a roof over our head and food in our mouth to survive and for this we need money. We may enjoy the trappings of luxury which indicate to others our worldly success. In our society, we tend to measure our worth by our possessions.

Many of us seek to express our identity through work and when our work is taken away — who are we? Where do we place ourselves in society? We often see ourselves through the eyes of others. When we believe others respect us, it means we have status. If we sense others are ridiculing us, we feel shame and anger and think of ourselves in a negative way. We believe that when we do our job of work, we are someone, others notice us, we have a place. When we have no work, we may feel lost, without purpose or not good enough to get by on the merit of our personality alone. We tend to judge ourselves and each other by what we have and what we do — not who we are.

We may seek to have power (financial or control over others) through our work. When this power is taken away from us, we may feel helpless.

Using career counselling

Some companies offer career counselling as part of the redundancy package. This may be a good option to take up or you could decide to use an external careers counsellor. The service may offer psychometric testing for assessing your interests, personality and skills together with guidance on refocusing your career direction and on training opportunities. At the very least, companies should offer you job-hunting time.

SAYING GOODBYE

The last few days

Some companies request that you leave the premises immediately you receive redundancy notice so that you don't affect other staff. Most companies, however, require some notice to be worked. This can be difficult. Motivation is low and feelings are high. You don't feel inclined to do your job which will make money for the company which is rejecting you. You may experience the bitterness of the "why me?" syndrome and want it to be someone else.

The time between when you know and when you go is bound to be tense. Ideally just working out your notice to the best of your ability and making the best of a bad situation is the easiest way through a very difficult situation. You may dream about taking your redundancy money and blowing it — for the first time in your life, you may have more money than you've ever had. Dream a little! And it's never too early to start looking for another job.

- *Checkpoint*
  It may be worth while negotiating to take a lump sum and leave rather than work out your notice.

Beginning to network

It is a good idea to begin developing contacts (networking) before you finally leave the company (or when you begin to hear rumours). Colleagues and management in particular can be useful. Networking is an invaluable key to your next job. Don't be shy of telling people you've been made redundant.

Be a floater
Accessing and sharing information with others.

Get a mentor
The definition of a mentor is someone who coaches and gives advice. To acquire a mentor you need to be seen to have qualities which suggest you are going somewhere.

Get sponsors
A sponsor is someone who promotes you to others. Being well perceived and possessing a high level of visibility are vital.

Network your boss
Assisting your boss to strengthen his/her network is likely to result in opportunities for you. Identify your boss's route of networking and get visibility on this route. Networking your boss to key personnel (inside and outside your company) should connect you with some vital people and give you extra opportunities.

- *Networking project*
  Draw up an organisational chart adding the names and job titles for your organisation or department.

DEALING WITH LOSS

Self assessment

Since being told you have been made redundant, are you experiencing:

a lack of personal fulfilment	.....	loss of status	.....
worry about your income	.....	loss of independence	.....
a change in lifestyle	.....	lack of community support	.....
fear about change	.....	anxiety about decision making	.....
an inability to share feelings	.....	family discord	.....
concurrent life crisis	.....	excessive activity	.....
depression (apathy, fatigue, withdrawal)	.....	feelings of alienation	.....
anger	.....	powerlessness	.....
guilt	.....	shame	.....
nervous anxiety	.....	physical ailments or illness	.....
self pity	.....	confusion and mood swings	.....

A combination of any of these could indicate that you are going through the grieving process. This process is where we honour the loss of job, status and friends amongst other things.

What do we lose?

Self esteem
Our sense of who we are, and our security surrounding our place in society, as defined through work, can feel threatened. We may feel shaky about our skills and knowledge. Weren't we good enough for the job? Are we good enough to get another job?

Dignity
Most of us develop a sense of pride in what we do for a living. There is a sense of ownership and attachment to what we have produced. When this living is taken away from us, we see the beliefs and values which we have attached to our work disappear.

Personal fulfilment
Work can provide a great deal of satisfaction. It affirms what we can do and what we know. It can affirm that we are needed. When work is no longer there, we may find it hard to find pleasure in more basic achievements.

Status
There may be feelings of shame attached to the label of redundant. Although nowadays there is more sympathy, there is still an ingrained sense of shame in the belief that we are not wanted. We take it as a personal affront, men in particular believing their identity is linked to their work.

Income
This is a major loss. If we don't have money, how will we eat, keep a roof over our heads and pay the bills? Linked to this is the loss of luxuries — the car, the holiday, the meals out. What will happen to the savings?

Independence
For many of us, work represents financial independence. It may also represent independence from the role of parent or carer. Work may be seen as a place where we can be expressive and free.

Lifestyle
Certain lifestyles can be connected with many jobs, *eg* sales or management. Overnight stays, company cars or entertaining are some of the perks we may lose when made redundant.

Property
When faced with redundancy, one of the major fears is the loss of our home. It may be that our home is linked directly with our job, *eg* caretaking or if we work for a bank. Even if our home is not directly linked, there is the threat of it being taken away if we don't keep up the mortgage repayments.

What complicates loss?

Lack of community support
One of the first questions we normally ask someone we first meet is 'what do you do'? If at that point we are not working, we may feel uncomfortable with this question. It is indicative of our society that we label each other by our work.

Change
Part of the human condition is a need to feel safe and secure. We do not mind change so much if we are in control, but when external circumstances force our hand, we tend to react with hostility and fear.

Anxiety about making decisions
When we are made redundant, we face the unknown. We have to make decisions about ourselves, what we want and how we are going to get it. Many of us fear making decisions because we don't want to make the wrong ones — so we don't make any and end up feeling lost and frustrated.

Inability to share feelings
Redundancy invariably produces an emotional reaction and emotions can be difficult to handle, especially if there is a lack of support or acceptance around us. If we are not happy with our own emotions, we tend to reject the emotions of others.

Family discord
At the time of losing our job, we may already be experiencing difficul-

ties in our personal relationships. Redundancy may make these communication problems even more pronounced.

Presence of concurrent life crises
Sometimes life seems to empty all the negative out at once. It may be that we are experiencing problems in other areas of our life and then just to cap it all along comes redundancy.

The grieving cycle

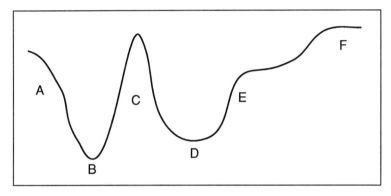

Fig. 1. The grieving cycle.

A The pattern of **life prior to redundancy**. During this time we may be advancing in our work and getting a sense of achievement. Or maybe we are hating our work or feeling uncomfortable with those we work with.

B The **loss and shock** due to redundancy with maybe a temporary numbness or disbelief. Some people may react with excessive activity, others with depression. There may be a feeling of unity with others in the company at the sense of loss. There may be feelings of alienation. The world stands still when we hear that we are being made redundant. We don't want to believe our world is falling apart. We don't want to believe that someone doesn't want us. We don't want to believe we are dispensable. We go blank. We may stay blank. We don't talk about it. We may immerse ourselves in activity so we don't think about it. We just can't believe it. Redundancy happens to other people. Not us. But it has happened and we have to deal with it somehow. We feel apart, alone, separate. We may not want to tell our family and friends — they have jobs, we don't. We may feel separate from colleagues at work who still have their jobs.

C **Emotional reaction** such as anger, powerlessness, guilt. We hang our heads, we hide away in shame. The great British stiff upper lip shows itself. Don't cry or shout, don't lose control because you've lost your job. Feeling powerless and out of control of our employment is a frightening state. We feel small, helpless and vulnerable, like a child again. Anger at your boss, at the company, the managing director, God, the government. Underlying anger which you feel at yourself may be redirected at your family. Anger turned inwards against the self can often turn into depression and apathy. Low self esteem and lack of confidence may evolve. Internal tension such as nervous anxiety may show itself. Psychosomatic ailments such as backache, headache or an illness may manifest. We feel self pity. With the confusion and mood swings that come with redundancy, we may not feel like exposing ourselves to the act of love-making.

D Onset of the **grieving process** where the reality of redundancy is experienced.

E **Change** where the loss is accepted and the idea of re-employment becomes a reality.

F **Rebuilding** a new working life.

Guidelines for healthy grieving

- to accept my sense of loss
- to let my feelings flow
- not to try and replace the loss immediately
- to let myself be with the pain of loss
- to talk to safe people about my feelings
- to take good care of myself
- to involve myself with meaningful activity
- to have fun
- to take the time I need.

Working with anger
Anger is a primary emotion following redundancy. It is fuelled by a

sense of frustration and powerlessness. It may also be a cover for fear and anxiety about the future.

Getting angry helps us to:

- discover what happened and what is happening to us
- set limits where necessary
- grieve for our losses
- get our needs met
- discover what is beneath our anger
- be assertive
- get things off our chest.

Repressed anger can cause:

- resentment
- self pity
- stress
- anxiety
- depression
- sadness
- lack of concentration
- physical illness.

Choices in handling anger

- smother it and experience numbness
- hold it in until it becomes resentment
- let it fester away inside until it becomes a physical illness
- displace the anger and cover it with work, eating, drugs or alcohol
- express it appropriately.

Expressing the anger appropriately

- grieve
- throw eggs in the bath
- punch a cushion
- scream into a pillow
- scream in your car with the windows wound up
- write an 'open letter' stating exactly how you feel (then keep it or burn it)

- tear up newspapers, magazines or the phone book
- cry.

Self evaluation of anger

1. If you do express anger, how do you do it? Are you aggressive, assertive, stubborn, complaining, rebellious?

2. Identify what you feel is being hurt and threatened by your anger.

3. Do you believe you have a right to be angry?

4. List specific examples of your behaviour that indicate you can express anger in a healthy way.

Making friends with fear

Fear can be a debilitating emotion. But it is natural and it is better to make a friend of fear and to work with it than to be afraid of fear itself.

We may fear:

- the loss of purpose and meaning in our lives
- the loss of job and material possessions
- unpredictability
- looking foolish
- loss of financial security
- changing a career
- being interviewed
- rejection
- failure
- loss of image
- helplessness
- the loss of status
- the unknown
- the loss of control
- change
- making decisions
- asserting oneself
- making a mistake
- success
- being vulnerable
- disapproval
- filling in forms

Questions we ask ourselves

- How will I financially survive?

- Am I too old to get a job?
- What will my friends say?
- Will my home be taken away?
- What will the neighbours say?
- Who else will want me?
- What will happen to me?
- How do I tell my partner?
- How do I pay my bills?
- What else can I do?

Low self esteem
When we experience low self esteem, we may:

- fear rejection
- fear failure
- need to be perfect
- appear incompetent
- have a negative self-image.

As our self esteem increases, we:

- become more confident
- express feelings
- take risks
- act more assertively.

COPING WITH THE FIRST FEW DAYS

Lazing around
We are so used to 'doing', we may find it hard to let go. The first few days or weeks after you have finished work, you may feel lost — without purpose. Try to use this time to create some space to have fun, to let go. It may be hard for the mind to stop, but it can be helpful to slow down and allow a sense of positive freedom to enter.

Catching up
You could use some of the time to catch up on those odd jobs. This may help with a sense of achievement and usefulness. You could:

- finish some household chores
- catch up on paperwork

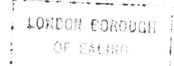

- do some DIY
- see old friends
- indulge your hobbies.

Nurture yourself

If we have lost our job, we can spend a lot of time mentally beating ourselves up. We forget to forgive ourselves, to take care of ourselves. If our best friend had lost their job, we would listen to them, be with them, help to cheer them up. So maybe we need to treat ourselves as our own best friend. We need to have fun, to nurture ourselves. Maybe you could:

- visit some interesting place

- buy yourself something special you can afford

- listen to soothing music

- listen to a positive and motivational tape

- make a special dinner for yourself and eat by candle-light

- write out an ideal scenario concerning a goal and visualise it

- write in a special journal about your accomplishments

- meditate.

Being with family and friends

Emotional support from family and partners is vital for you to feel valued and accepted. It is good to have special people who will hug and hold you and who will listen to you.

Your thought process

Our thought process gives rise to our reality in life. If we have negative beliefs, we experience negative outcomes in life. When we experience positive self talk, we then have a good chance of experiencing the best that life can offer.

One way in which we can identify negative beliefs is by managing four different parts of our nature that send us messages:

- **The critic**
  'What a disappointment you are —'
  'You can't provide for your family —'

- **The perfectionist**
  'You should —'
  'You must —'

- **The worrier**
  'What if —'
  'We won't have a roof over our heads —'

- **The victim**
  'I'll never be able to get another job —'
  'No one wants me —'

We may have further negative beliefs that come from our past such as:

- I must not show anger
- I must keep a stiff upper lip
- I can't handle rejection
- They don't appreciate me
- It's my fault
- I must not seem vulnerable
- I can't handle uncertainty
- They've got no right to get rid of me
- I'm not good enough
- I must always be working.

Using mind power

1. Create a mental image for your doubting side:
   eg a thin, black creature pointing accusingly.

2. Create a mental image for your reinforcing side:
   eg an all wise male dressed in white with a flowing beard.

3. What negative messages is your doubting side saying?
   eg 'no one wants your skills'.

4. What positive messages can your reinforcing side say?
   eg 'my skills are useful and I keep adding to them'.

List your positives

- 6 x qualities I like about myself
- 2 x times I have felt loved
- 2 x times I have been congratulated
- 2 x difficulties I handle well
- 4 x responsibilities I shoulder successfully.

Beginning your new routine

- get up at a regular time
- exercise
- network with colleagues and friends
- socialise
- improve your image
- reorganise your finances
- do voluntary/community work
- get out and about
- write your CV
- get in touch with agencies
- redefine personal goals
- return to study
- redefine career goals

CHECKLIST FOR THE FIRST FEW WEEKS

1. See redundancy as a positive opportunity for change.

2. Allow yourself time to grieve and say goodbye.

3. Express your anger appropriately.

4. Write out your feelings.

5. Can your life or health cover continue after you leave?

6. Put your financial package in a high interest account.

7. Could you negotiate a lump sum and leave rather than work out your notice?

8. Organise networking contacts before you leave.

9. Keep busy.

10. Look after yourself.

11. Have some fun.

CASE STUDIES

Angela's choice
Angela Black is 42, married with two teenage children and has worked for a building society for 12 years. She has held a variety of administration posts in the company and has spent the past three years working as a personal assistant for one of the management. Her post is being swallowed up by another department and she has been given the choice of moving yet again to another post within the company or taking voluntary redundancy. There had been rumours for some time before the official announcement. She has decided to take redundancy with a large financial package after working one month's notice. Now she is contemplating possible choices with enthusiasm, although she felt sad at leaving so many friends.

Robert is waiting to leave
Robert Clark had always wanted to be a printer and completed a five year apprenticeship after leaving school. Redundancy comes after 15 years of working for the same company. There had been growing discontent in the company and at 33 Robert wasn't sure whether to leave voluntarily or to hang on for possible redundancy. He is married with no children and dislikes change, especially when forced upon him. He decides to hang on for redundancy, which does happen. He has two weeks notice to work out and is insecure and anxious about his future. He feels sad at having to leave good work-mates and angry with his feelings of powerlessness.

Alan's new career path
Alan Withers had worked his way up to management in advertising and marketing and has found himself made redundant for the third time. At 52, divorced and ambitious, he is no longer prepared to have other peo-

ple dictate his career path. His stress levels are high and he is experiencing strong feelings of bitterness and frustration.

DISCUSSION POINTS

1. What do you think were the motivations behind the way in which you were informed of your redundancy — what alternative method could have been used, if any?

2. Define the influences that society has had on your personal perceptions of work.

3. Analyse how your particular career path has changed over the years and what has affected your choices.

2
Handling your Finances

ORGANISING YOUR FINANCES

Payments you are entitled to when made redundant
Your employer should pay:

- any wages you are owed

- holiday pay (for holidays you are entitled to but haven't taken)

- in lieu of notice if you have not been given the proper period of notice

- redundancy payment.

Your redundancy package is likely to include **financial compensation**. At this point, it may be tempting to go out and blow the lot. The sensible short-term policy would be to put it into a high-interest account in the building society or bank, dream a little, then after some distance is put between your turbulent emotions and your money — take rational action.

An employer must make a lump sum payment to an employee made redundant, provided the employee has at least two years' continuous service for at least 16 hours a week or if they have been employed continuously for five years for at least eight hours a week. Service before the age of 18 and after 64 does not count. If you have been made redundant, you may not be entitled to payment if a new job is offered with the same employer or a successor employer who takes over the business, provided the new job is offered before the old employment contract expires and you start within four weeks.

The amount of your redundancy payment depends on how long you have been continuously employed by your employer, how the years of service relate to particular age bands and on weekly pay:

Age 41-65   one and a half weeks' pay for each complete year of employment
Age 22-41   one week's pay for each complete year of employment
Age 18-22   half a week's pay for each complete year of employment.

If you have lost your job and your former employer owes you money which the company cannot pay because of insolvency, the Employment Department may be able to settle the debts, or part of them. Self employed people do not qualify. The main debts you can claim include: any wages you are owed, holiday pay and compensation for financial loss you may have suffered by not being given a proper period of notice or pay in lieu of notice.

Title	Code	From
A guide to income support	IB20	DSS
A guide to housing benefit	RR2	DSS
Which benefit?	FB2	DSS
One parent benefit	CH11	DSS
Help with the Council Tax	CTB1	DSS
Mortgage interest direct	IS8	DSS
Family credit claim pack	FC1	DSS
Unemployment benefit	N112	DSS
Redundancy payments	PL 808	Employment Department

Fig. 2. Benefit leaflet guide.

Checkpoints for your redundancy package

- Can you retain your company car for a while?

- Could you purchase your company car at a favourable rate?

- Can you negotiate the continuation of life or health insurance cover for a short time after you leave?

- Is there payment for career counselling or outplacement assistance?

Handling your Finances

- Are you owed holiday pay?

- What happens to your pension?

Using your redundancy money
Make your money work for you:

- pay off any hire purchase

- don't rush into buying a business

- don't take the first person's advice that you speak to

- don't be speculative

- check to see if your loan agreement has any insurance cover against unemployment

- put your money into a high interest account until you have had the best advice.

Organising your personal budget

- keep outgoings minimal
- look at your expenditure
- you may be able to take a private pension from age 50
- your work pension is likely to be frozen
- keep your life insurance going.

Using the benefit system
Your redundancy payment does not affect your entitlement to unemployment benefit. For advice and information on benefits, talk to a claimant adviser at the Jobcentre.

Checkpoints

- Doing voluntary work should not affect your benefit as long as you are still actively searching for work.

- If you have a mortgage, see your building society or bank to discuss rescheduling your repayments.

MONTHLY OUTGOING	AMOUNT	MONTHLY INCOMING	AMOUNT
rent/mortgage		salary — spouse	
council tax		unemployment benefit	
water rates		building society interest	
house/contents insurance		child allowance	
life insurance		severance pay	
electricity		retirement income	
gas		share dividends	
telephone			
car			
public transport			
savings			
food			
newspapers/subscriptions			
your clothes			
children's clothes			
cigarettes			
birthdays/Christmas			
meals out/alcohol			
holidays			
loans			
TV rental/licence			
household			
credit cards			
HP			
childcare			
health insurance			
Total		Total	

Fig. 3. Your budget plan.

YOUR LOW COST OR NO COST LIFESTYLE

Gardening
Tidying up and weeding cost nothing. If you're in the season of cuttings, ask your friends and neighbours for a free sample.

Decorating and home furnishings
Four tins of paint and you can transform a room. If you don't want to paint, give the paintwork a good washdown instead, cost — only soap and water. Don't always think just about the purchase price of an appliance, consider how much it costs to run. Consider energy saving around the home. Consider buying your furnishings from auctions.

Your car
If you are thinking of buying another car, consider how much it will depreciate in the first year and what else you could do with that money. Using diesel in your car is cheaper than petrol. Unleaded petrol is cheaper than leaded. The higher the gear the lower your fuel consumption. The heavier the car the more fuel it will take to move it. If waiting in a queue for longer than two minutes turn off your engine to conserve energy. Driving at lower speeds will reduce fuel consumption.

Food and drink
Invest in a home brew kit. The outlay is minimal and you can have lots of fun preparing brews of cider, wine and beer. If you don't want to buy the ready made kits, you can make home brew from almost anything in your garden or kitchen cupboard. Ask your friendly greengrocer for the vegetables or fruit they normally throw away. Try not to spend too much on convenience foods. Don't be put off by plain packaging if the product is cheap.

Entertainment and holidays
Go for a walk in the country, visit the local pub for a drink and a snack, have fish and chips. Visit a museum, browse in a music or book shop, take a scenic drive, go to the beach, walk on a scenic path in the park. Hiring a video is cheaper than going to the cinema. Look out for free concerts advertised in

	the local paper. When eating out a set menu is cheaper than a la carte. Consider late availability holidays from travel agents or a house swap for a cheap holiday. Rent a house with friends for the summer break.
Clothes	Oxfam do a great deal on business suits these days. Alternatively wait for the sales, have a swop shop with friends or, if handy with a needle and thread, revamp your own.
Keep fit	Run round the block, walk everywhere, exercise with a friend.
Nurturing yourself	Go to a children's playground and use the swings, have an ice cream or lolly, play with a child as if you were a peer, read a comic or annual, climb a tree, play football, play frisbee, watch kiddies' TV, play snap, see a funny video, meditate, call a good friend, play music, relax with a good book, work on a puzzle book, write a letter to a special person.
Get physical	Take a sauna or a warm bubble bath, sing, dance, walk barefoot, sleep outside under the stars, go to bed early, watch the sunrise or sunset, smell some flowers, get a massage, float in water.
Philosophy	Popularity, self expression, self respect, honesty, loyalty, intimacy, inner security, a sense of purpose, laughter, love, comfort, challenge — none of these cost anything.

DEFINING YOUR NEEDS AND WANTS

It is easier to look at what others want and need instead of looking inside ourselves. We are often taught to ignore our own needs and focus on others. Society and conditioning contribute to what we believe we must have in order to be happy. Of course we need a roof over our head and food in our mouth, but there are many appendages we believe we cannot survive without.

Needs are associated with what humans require for their physical survival. According to the psychologist Abraham Maslow, there are five levels of human needs:

- Physiological needs — food, water, sleep, oxygen

- Safety needs — shelter, stable environment, income

- Belongingness — support from others, a sense of belonging

- Esteem needs — self-respect, skill, status, a sense of accomplishment

- Self actualisation — fulfilment of your potential in life, self determination.

Projects

1. Make two separate lists — the ten things you most want to do and the ten things you most often do. Compare.

2. Spend a whole day paying attention to how many times you say 'I want' or 'I need'. What do you want and need?

3. Take ten blank postcards and write on each card 'What I need is —' and complete the phrase without judgement. Take another ten postcards and write on each card 'What I want is —' and complete the phrase without judgement. Prioritise each section. What do they tell you?

REDEFINING YOUR MATERIAL VALUES

Most of us seek attachment to the external world via money, our home, a car and other possessions. We believe that our survival depends on us having these things. We believe that our possessions are a gauge of who we are and whether we are accepted by others.

Some of us are ruled by what we see as the importance of money: 'others will like me if I have lots of money' or 'If I had more money, I could do more things/buy more things and then I would be happy'.

- We are fearful about money. If we don't have enough, we are afraid that we won't have what we need. If we are rich, we are afraid of losing it. We may have lots of money but feel guilty about it or we may have less and feel resentful about it. In the area of work and money you may have to be willing to take risks. If you do only what you think you should in order to earn a living, then you won't be listening to your inner voice that tells you what you really need to do. Our hopes and fears around money tend to come from our conditioning as seen through the eyes of our first family.

Negative beliefs about money

- I don't have enough money

- I won't be able to pay my bills

- It's selfish to have money when others don't have enough.

Positive beliefs about money

- I deserve to be prosperous and happy

- There is plenty for everyone

- The more I prosper, the more I can share with others.

Self assessment

1. Reflect on the things you believe you need to have in your life and list ten things that you feel are indispensible to your well-being.

2. Tick those needs you feel are not being met right now.

3. List ten things you most want. Brainstorm without judgement.

4. Tick those wants that you feel you deserve. Compare how deserving you feel with how difficult you think your wants are to obtain.

5. Compare the two lists of wants and needs. On a separate sheet, put your two lists in descending order of importance. Note any changes.

In summary, if you organise **sensible budgeting**, money should be no problem. You may have to tighten the belt a little and not indulge in luxuries as you used to. But the good times will come back with a little patience and forethought. You may see your redundancy money as a safety net, you may use it to pay off some debt or it might give you the opportunity to make changes you've always wanted — and change is what redundancy is offering you.

CASE STUDIES

Angela invests in her future
Angela takes redundancy offering a large financial package after working one month's notice. With her investment knowledge, she places most of her money in a high interest account. She puts £2,000 in her current account — ready for more immediate treats for her family and herself. Some of her redundancy money will go towards moving house (her current house is tied to her place of work), some may go towards investing in her own business. Both her teenage children are working and contributing to the household expenses.

Robert tightens his belt
Robert takes a redundancy package of £13,000 including holiday pay and opens a current account in his local building society. His wife is earning and there are no outstanding debts to pay off apart from a credit card which they clear. Together they work out a financial belt-tightening strategy.

Alan's new career path
Alan has several nest eggs tucked away in various accounts plus some shares. He receives a financial package including a favourable price on his company car which he purchases. He cashes in some shares to keep going.

DISCUSSION POINTS

1. How were your family finances handled when you were a child?

2. Evaluate your attitude towards material possessions.

3. What would you like to change about your attitude towards money?

3
Making Changes

COPING WITH CHANGE

Most of us have a need to feel in control. When we instigate change, we feel in control, but redundancy happens to us — outside of our control. This can produce a reaction of feeling angry and overwhelmed. We need to regain some sense of control in order to cope with the enforced change. We can do this by:

- managing our time to explore and plan our life
- learning how to relax and nurture ourselves
- positive thinking
- looking after our health.

Other ways of helping ourselves cope with change include:

- getting as much information as possible about our situation
- learning the skills of decision making and goal setting
- networking
- expressing our feelings constructively.

There is nothing so constant as change, the saying goes. Change can bring fear and uncertainty but it can also bring fresh challenge and new opportunities.

Try completing — truthfully — the chart in Figure 4 and then make an effort to increase the good elements and cut down on the bad.

	Yes	Sometimes	No
Physical well-being			
I have a balanced daily diet of proteins and fibre			
My weight is appropriate for my age and height			
I drink at least three litres of water per day			
I drink no more than two pints of beer or two measures of spirits/wine daily			
I regularly smoke more than ten cigarettes a day			
I take care of my appearance			
I walk at least two miles a day			
I take part in non-competitive games or sport on a weekly basis			
I practise deep breathing/relaxation			
I spend regular time in the fresh air			
Mental and emotional well-being			
I have close friends			
I ask for support when I need it			
I give myself treats			
I have interests which enable me to learn new skills			
I have a sense of self-direction			
I have a good image of myself			
I can let go appropriately			
I am emotionally secure			

Fig. 4. Looking after yourself.

LOOKING AFTER YOUR HEALTH

Coping with the transition of change isn't easy. Although redundancy can give us a positive outcome, the process of arriving at that outcome can cause us stress. Therefore we need to have at our fingertips all the coping strategies we can, including stress and time management.

Both of these techniques have much to offer other areas of our lives as well as in career management. When we have a secure base within, we are in better shape to go out into the world. Looking after our mind and body, being selective over how we use our time, cultivating a positive attitude and exploring our work values and motivations can only have a beneficial effect on us and our career development.

Managing your stress

Stress is caused, not by an event, but by your response to the event. If you can control your levels of response, you can control stress. If you cannot change the environment, then you must change yourself and the perception of the event. Psychologists have suggested there are two types of responses to stress:

- Type A — Impatient, aggressive, driven, distorted sense of time, fast talker and mover. High risk of heart problems. The positive interpretation of this type of response could be — expressive, in control and sociable.

- Type B — Relaxed, unhurried, non-competitive and non-aggressive. The negative of this type of response could be — over-controlled and inhibited.

Project

Identify situations which you find personally stressful:

work	home	social	other	your coping strategy

Making Changes

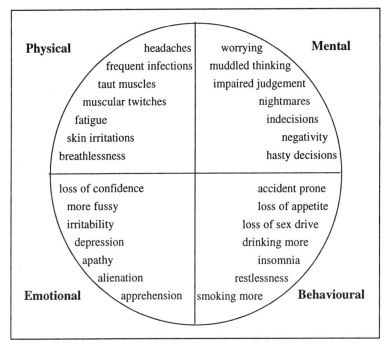

Fig. 5. Signs of stress.

Developing your security zones

Security zones are places, things or routines in your life which represent security and safety to you. They are areas of your life which are under your control or don't change.

What are your security zones?

Home	Beach
A favourite chair	Comfy clothes
Walking the dog	Reading
Watching old films	Hobbies
Talking to friends	Holidays
Sunday outings	The hairdresser
Friday night down the pub	Pets
The morning cup of tea	Gardening
Your favourite restaurant	Eating

Watching cartoons   Sleeping
A favourite room   Having a bath
The weekly shopping   Cuddling

Using relaxation techniques

Relaxation exercise
You could get someone to read this exercise to you or you could record it for yourself, speaking clearly and slowly. Wear loose clothing and find yourself a quiet, safe space where there are no telephones and you won't be interrupted. Sit in a comfy chair, lie on the bed or rest on the floor, with or without a cushion. The idea is not to go to sleep, but to change your level of consciousness to a more relaxed and peaceful state.

When you feel comfortable, close your eyes and become aware of your body, starting with your scalp. Feel your scalp relaxing, imagine someone is soothing back your hair and stroking all the tension away. Relax the forehead, raise the eyebrows and then lower them again, feeling the frown ease away. Feel the eyelids gently shut. Relax the facial muscles. Unclench the jaw. Wiggle the jaw from side to side and feel the tension ease away. Your tongue should be behind the lower teeth. Let your attention go to your throat and neck. Feel the tension easing. Imagine all the tension in your forehead and scalp going out of the base of your skull into infinity.

Move your attention down to your upper chest, feeling the muscles relax. Move your shoulders down and back, feel them relaxing into the chair, bed or floor. Move your attention to your left shoulder, relaxing the upper arm and the lower arm, feeling the tension flow into your left hand and out of your fingertips into infinity. Move your attention over to your right shoulder, relaxing the upper arm and the lower arms, feeling the tension flow into your right hand and out of your fingertips into infinity. Move your attention round to your back as it rests against the chair, floor or bed. Feel the tension easing in your upper back and your lower back. Feel the tension from your forehead, scalp and back drain down your spine and out of the small of your back into infinity. Move your awareness round to your stomach and feel the muscles relax and ease.

Relax your upper thighs and your calves, feeling the tension in your hips and legs flow into both feet and out of your soles into infinity. You are becoming more and more relaxed. More and more peaceful. There is nothing to do, nothing to change, just relax — relax — relax — relax.

Making Changes

Deep breathing
When you are in a stressed state, the breathing becomes shallow. Deep breathing can help to relax and focus the thoughts. The idea is to expand the stomach and rib cage, thereby using your entire lung capacity. You **inhale slowly and deeply** and **exhale even more slowly.**

Lie down in a comfortable position and place one hand either side of the stomach, fingers facing each other. As you inhale, make a concentrated effort to raise the stomach and feel your fingers expand. Slowly exhale completely. Now inhale for a count of five and exhale for a count of six. Do this five more times. Still with your hands on your stomach, inhale for a count of three, feeling the stomach rise. Now place one hand either side of your rib cage, fingers facing in. Continue to inhale for a count of seven, feeling the rib cage expand outwards. Now slowly exhale completely for a count of ten. Repeat five times.

Further stress-busting ideas

meditate	laugh	cry	slow down
do yoga	exercise	shout	make love
shrug it off	punch a cushion	write it out	detach from it

Face, head and neck massage

Self massage can help relieve muscle tension, easing the muscles into movement and stimulating the blood supply. Any one of the following may help ease tension:

1. Close your eyes and place the palms of each hand over your eye socket. You should find the result very restful.

2. Move your fingers along the edge of your skull from your ears towards the spine, and continue down the spine as far as you can. Then push the back neck muscles up towards your head.

3. Put your left hand on your right shoulder and roll the back muscle up and forward. Repeat with your right hand on your left shoulder.

4. Move your scalp over your skull with your fingertips.

Eating the healthy way

We are not talking diet but an all round health eating regime, which, without you even trying, will be low in fat, high in fibre and should result in you being the right weight. Ultimately a little of what you fancy does you good. There is not point in eating and drinking all the right things if you die of boredom along the way. A general guide could be:

- limit your intake of salt

- bananas, kiwi fruit, celery, grapes, lettuce, cinnamon, barley, brewer's yeast, oats, and basil are good soothers for stress levels

- increase your intake of low fat foods such as pasta, bread, white meat, vegetables, fruit and salad

- minimise intake of sugar and refined carbohydrates

- if you have low blood sugar, you will need a high protein/low carbohydrate diet with small, frequent meals

- alcohol, antibiotics, coffee, tea and sleeping pills destroy Vitamin B which is vital to the nervous system

- garlic, pumpkin seeds and sunflower seeds are good pep-ups

- avocado, lentils, raspberries and spinach are good for fatigue

- ginseng is a well known nutrient for stress (Siberian for the mind and Korean for the physical)

- calcium, magnesium, zinc, Vitamin B and C complex are beneficial for the nervous system.

Rest and recreation

We all need to play, sleep, dream and slob out from time to time. This provides us with the space to recharge our batteries and build up our reserves. It may even be, in these quiet times, that creative solutions to our problems occur.

USING POSITIVE THINKING

There is now plenty of scientific documentation demonstrating how the mind affects the body. When under severe or prolonged stress, the immune system doesn't function at optimum and it is the immune system which keeps infection and illness at bay. If we are in a negative

Making Changes

emotional or mental state, this can affect our physical well-being, thereby leading to disease.

A healthy mind is equal to a healthy body — the more positive we feel, the more healthy we are. The power of positive thinking not only affects our bodies, but also our experiences in life. What we think and how we feel produce the choices we make available to ourselves. From these choices, we make decisions and from these come our life experiences. Two techniques used to access positive thinking are **visualisations** and **affirmations**.

Visualisation
To visualise is to use our mind's eye. We can see in our mind a person close to us even though we are not with them, we can visualise our favourite food or replay our favourite film.

Exercise
Sit or lie down in a quiet, comfortable place and go through your relaxation and deep breathing exercise. Try to visualise what your stress looks like, *eg* a tightly squeezed cloth, sharp teeth or turbulent waves. Now imagine the opposite, *eg* gently rippling silk, smooth curves or still water.

Affirmations
Affirmation means 'to make firm'. An affirmation is a short statement, written or spoken, which affirms the positive. It is always worded in the present and reinforces the good that you want.

Exercise
Take a sheet of paper and write down some positive affirmations, *eg* relax, calm down, take it easy or I can relax and let go. Write each one out 15 times in succession. Try using your name to prefix it, *eg* I, Mick, can relax and let go.

MANAGING YOUR TIME

The art of time management is the effective organisation of the hours available to you. Whether it be at work, home or play, it is satisfying to know you have made the best use of your time. For effective time management to occur, the following needs to happen:

Establishing clear and realistic objectives
You need to establish what you want and why. You need to establish

your work motivations and personal value system in order to redefine your career direction. There needs to be realistic objectives set out for your career development.

Planning and prioritising
As your thoughts and ideas become clearer, you need to begin making plans for a jobsearch strategy. You need to prioritise activities for two reasons: first to achieve your objectives and secondly to give yourself motivation.

Problem solving
Effective time management during your jobsearch includes problem solving. This means being able to think laterally, to find another way in when a door closes in your face. Problem solving skills include knowing where to find information, who and what to ask.

Assertiveness
Managing your time often means saying no or maybe saying yes. Your time is valuable. It represents space for yourself. Time to think. Time for action. Other people may intrude on this and you need to be able to say assertively what you need to happen. Being assertive means respecting your rights to define yourself while respecting the rights of others to do the same. Being passive means letting others use you. Being aggressive means you use others. Being assertive means self respect, valuing your time and effort and asking others to respect your wishes.

Letting go
There are only so many hours in a day to do things, to see other people and to be with yourself. Sometimes, you need to say goodbye — to let go of something or someone in order to make room for new growth. Your redundancy was an enforced goodbye. Maybe, as you review your life, there are other goodbyes to make.

Decision making
It is better to make a decision which may be bad than not to do anything at all and live to regret it. Successful time management involves making decisions, accepting responsibility for them and seeing them through. Dithering wastes time and takes up mental effort needlessly. We tend to put off making decisions because we are afraid of failure or appearing stupid. But if we make a mistake, we learn, and if we have self respect,

how can we look stupid? What we think of ourselves is more important than how we believe (often wrongly) others are seeing us.

Major time wasters

interruptions	the telephone	crisis
junk mail	poor reading skills	procrastination
comfortable jobs	social chat	addiction to adrenaline
travel	lack of planning	lack of innovation
not finishing things	feeling guilty	lack of confidence
insecurity	over-tight schedules	showing off
need to be liked	identity crisis	reluctance to confront
not listening	pretending to know	talking too much
need to be in control	can't say no	poor sense of time
laziness	poor rapport skills	fatigue
forgetting	dishonesty	jealousy

What do **you** do to waste time?

Guidelines for successful time management

- Prioritise
- Don't waste time
- Set your goals
- Plan
- Delegate and work with others
- Manage your stress and health
- Review.

Make two copies of the time management diary in Figure 6. Complete one copy with the activities of an ordinary day, then fill in the second copy with a plan of what you **need** to do — and compare the two.

Project

Get a piece of paper and head up three columns: 1 = Priority, 2 = Important and 3 = Can wait. Place all the things you want to do under whichever column seems appropriate. Then put the 2 column into either the 1s or 3s. Now start doing the 1s and leave the 3s for later.

Time	Activity description
6.00	
6.30	
7.00	
7.30	
8.00	
8.30	
9.00	
9.30	
10.00	
10.30	
11.00	
11.30	
Mid-Day	
12.30	
1.00	
1.30	
2.00	
2.30	
3.00	
3.30	
4.00	
4.30	
5.00	
5.30	
6.00	
6.30	
7.00	
7.30	
8.00	
8.30	
9.00	

Fig. 6. Your time management diary.
Fill this in for one day and see what kind of activities are useful and which waste time.

Self evaluation of making changes			
What I would like to achieve	The obstacles	My fears	Support I need

CASE STUDIES

Angela's philosophy
Angela feels ready for change and believes in making the best of things. She has a fatalistic attitude towards life and is ready to try anything, feeling that when the right thing comes along, she would know it. She relaxes with friends and reads. She switches off emotionally and escapes into a philosophical approach.

Robert's anxiety
Robert is an intense man who is emotionally passionate. He stores up anger easily and takes rejection very personally. During the time just prior to his redundancy and just following it, he and his wife take time to talk about his thoughts and feelings. He feels insecure and anxious about change, but talking helps to release some of the pressure and his health during that time stayed good apart from a slight cold. He starts to go jogging around this time.

Alan's new career path

Alan is driven by a desire to succeed and to be seen as a success. He realises change is necessary but feels resentful about having to even consider it. He keeps going to his health club which he uses to release his stress levels. He has an ulcer and a great deal of muscular tension.

DISCUSSION POINTS

1. How might occupational stress manifest itself within the working environment?

2. Explore how external changes (company, family, economic) have affected your career development so far.

3. Research any possible connections between your health (or that of someone close to you) and the events in your (in their) life. Have there been times when stress and ill health have coincided?

4
Re-defining your Value System

WHY WORK?

When I asked six youngsters around the age of 17 what they would do if they had a £1,000 cheque given to them every week for doing absolutely nothing, they all said they would go and find something to do — otherwise they would be bored. I asked the same question of six adults between 25 and 45 and most of them said they would do nothing. The difference in attitude was revealing — and a little sad.

We need to have some motivation to achieve anything in life. We need to have a reason, a payoff, otherwise we see no reason for making an effort. For example, our motivations to get up and make a cup of tea could be thirst, boredom, hunger, anxiety or the need to take a pill.

In order to enjoy our work, what are our motivations? The three main motivations are status, money and power. Status, in order to have a personal sense of identity or to be recognised by others. Money, for a roof over our head and food in our mouths. We may have a dependent family. We like money for luxuries. Then comes power — money brings power and status brings power. We may feel power over work colleagues or subordinates, we may feel power over fate, God, the government or the system.

Work can be a drudgery if you have been doing something that does not represent the real you. It can build resentment and frustration. During times of recession, employers hold the winning hand and may deliberately create an environment of fear to keep at bay the pay claims. If you don't feel valued or appreciated, this can wear away at the human spirit, leaving morale and motivation low.

To be realistic, we are not going to be happy in our work all of the time, nor are we going to like everyone we work with nor is everyone going to like us. But we do have the right to enjoy our work and to use and develop our skills as much as possible.

Work purpose self assessment

- How can I begin taking steps toward discovering and doing work that would be personally meaningful?
- Would I like to return to study or training to improve my career path?
- What are my most important values with regard to career achievement?
- Is material success my main motivation for why I work?

Mark the following out of five for how true you think it is. Work:

— is something I do for money
— helps me get up in the morning
— takes me away from the family
— gives my life structure
— gives me an identity
— gives me a social life
— provides me with a sense of purpose
— provides me with interesting challenges
— makes me feel needed
— gives me status
— is unenjoyable
— is boring.

What do you miss by not working?

The bridge of life

Each of us goes through cycles in life. Broadly speaking, the cycles correspond to ages and to a greater or lesser extent, we all share the cycles.

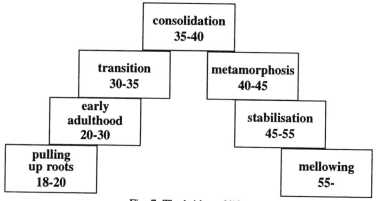

Fig. 7. The bridge of life.

Pulling up roots	—	leaving the nest, flexing the wings to express individuality, realising that there are different ways of being
Early adulthood	—	first commitments to adult responsibilities, trying out parental rules in the world, early mistakes
Transition	—	re-examination of parental rules, reassessment of current relationships and career, challenges to our old ways of thinking, more long-term planning beginning to occur
Consolidation	—	seeking to become established, the beginning of feeling pressurised by time, making long-term goals based on our true individuality and not on family expectations
Metamorphosis	—	facing the chasm between ideals and reality, new career, new relationships, breaking down, breaking away
Stabilisation	—	increased stability following changes
Mellowing	—	achievement losing potency in the face of increased self satisfaction and inner peace with self.

My work values and motivations

Your value system gives shape to your life experiences. Your values are mostly in your subconscious and are formed by society and early family conditioning. Values may originate from your parents or society or elsewhere. You may share them or you may be carrying them around with you, believing they are your own. This exercise represents your personal needs behind your job choice. Go through the list, marking those values that are important to you.

accomplishment	attention to detail	being a team member
activity	autonomy	being appreciated
a sense of community	being a success	being efficient

being expert	identity	stress
being of service	independence	supervising others
being outdoors	influence	supporting others
being precise	irregular hours	taking risks
being supervised	loyalty	time freedom
belonging	making decisions	to be indoors
change	meeting deadlines	to be pro-active
communication	mostly sitting	to motivate others
competitiveness	mostly standing	to organise
contentment	overcoming challenges	tranquility
creativity	overtime perks	travel
developing new skills	pleasing others	usefulness
discipline	precise work	using existing skills
dressing casual	pressure	using lots of energy
dressing well	promotion	using my intellect
earning commission	public contact	wisdom
excitement	recognition	working alone
fast pace	regular hours	working close to home
financial security	respect from others	working in a large business
gaining knowledge	routine	working in a small business
having authority	self development	working in the country
having feedback	self respect	working with others
having responsibility	sense of purpose	
having support	social interaction	
helping society	status	

What kind of person am I?
How would I assess myself?
Strong points: _____
Weak areas: _____

Self assessment
Who are you? Who or what we believe ourselves to be is relevant to how we perceive ourselves out in the world. Write down without thinking, who or what you believe yourself to be at this point in time.
I am a person who:

Project: Where am I at?
Reflect upon this period in your life and ask yourself 'Where am I at in my life right now?' Think about what kind of time this is for you. Consider the event or events which have marked the beginning of this period and think about the chief characteristics of this period. Is it a hectic time? A time of crisis? A period of transition? A stagnant period? Draw any images, colours, forms or write any words or statements that reflect where you are in your life at this particular time.

My career needs and wants
What we need and want in our work may be one and the same. What we want is desirable but not essential to our well-being. What we need is vital to our sense of self. Complete the following and find out what the difference is for you.

1. I want
    eg stimulation, stable income for emotional security, to create something of substance and for a reason, to be challenged, a higher income, a sense of belonging.

2. I need
    eg to contribute to household expenses, to be doing something useful, to be more independent, to be needed, to develop new skills.

3. What will happen if I don't have it?
    eg I will feel trapped, useless, bored and frustrated.

4. What could I begin to do to remedy the situation?
    eg re-train, consider more permanent positions offering autonomy.

ASSESSING YOUR SKILLS

Checkpoint

- **What am I good at?**
  What we are good at isn't necessarily what we want to do.

- **What would I like to learn?**
  If we don't know how to do something, how do we know if we might be good at it?

Look through the following list and put one tick by what you think you are good at and two ticks by what you would like to learn:

accounting
acting
acupuncturist
administration
advertising
agriculture
ambulance driver
animal training
antiques
archaeology
architecture
archive work
armed forces
aromatherapy
art and design
art evaluation
assembling things
auctioneering
author
banking
beautician
bookbinding
book-keeping
breeding animals
brewer
broadcasting
building furniture
building society
building work
calculating
career guidance
caring for animals
carpentry
cartography
catering
chartered secretary
childcare
chiropodist

chiropractic
church work
cleaning
clerical
clinical psychology
coaching a sport
coastguard
community work
composing music
computer work
construction
consumer protection
conservation
contract management
copywriting
corporate planning
counselling
courier
court work
craft projects
creating clothes
customs work
dancing
demolition worker
dentistry
designing jewellery
designing posters etc.
diagnostics
dietician
diplomatic work
director
display work
dog handler
drama coach
draughtsperson
drawing plans
dressmaker
driving instructor

economic analysis
editor
education
electrics
electronics
engineering
environmental health
factory inspector
farming
fashion modelling
film direction
finance consultancy
fisheries work
flight operations
floral design
forestry
food preparation
forensic science
forestry
fund-raising
furniture restoration
gourmet cooking
graphic designer
groom
growing fruit/veg
hairdressing
herbalism
holiday guide
homeopath
horticulture
hotel work
house repairs
house restoration
hydrography
hydrology
industrial relations
information provider
insurance

Re-defining your Value System

installation	pharmacy	shiatsu
interior design	photography	shipping
inventing	physiotherapy	sign writer
investment mngt.	picture framing	silversmith
journalism	piloting	singer
lab technician	planning routes	site engineer
landscape gardening	plants/animals	social sciences
lecturing	playgroup work	social services
legal services	playwright	social worker
librarianship	plumbing	solving crime
machine operation	police work	speech therapy
machine supervision	politics	sport
management	printing	statistics
mngt consultancy	prison service	stockbroking
marketing	probation	storage/delivery
market research	production mngt.	surgeon
massage	project engineer	surveying
mechanical repairs	property dev.	systems
mechanics	public relations	tax work
medical administration	public spokesperson	taxi driver
merchant banking	publishing	teaching
metallurgy	quality control	technical writing
meterology	quantity surveying	telephone work
mining	radiography	town planning
museum work	recreation management	training
musician	reflexology	traffic operations
natural science	repairing	translator
nursing	research	transport management
occupational therapy	research scientist	typography
office work	restoring textile items	undertaker
optician	retail management	upholsterer
organise trips/events	riding instructor	vehicle maintenance
osteopath	secretary	vet
painting/decorating	security	waitress
performing	selling	woodworker
personnel	selling plants	youth worker
pharmacology	servicing	

The skills you put one tick by:

__ how extensive is your experience?

— would you like to work in this area?
— could you make a sideways move in this area?
— would further training enhance your prospects?
— why do you want to work in this area?

The skills you put two ticks by:

— would you return to part-time study to learn this?
— would you return to full-time study to learn this?
— why do you want to work in this area?
— what do you know about this area?
— what are the prospects?

YOUR IDEAL CAREER

You are to imagine that there are no constraints of money, age, or health. Identify details such as job specification, with whom would you work, in what kind of surroundings, with what kind of authority and responsibilities, with what kind of working day. Detail career progression and income sought, opportunities for using your present skills and developing others.

Now think through the following:

- What does the fantasy indicate about what I would value and aspire to?

- What are the differences between fantasy and my reality?

- How much of my fantasy is achievable at the present or might be in the future?

- What are the barriers to my achieving some of my fantasy and how might these be overcome?

- What would be the consequences of my working to achieve some of the features of my fantasy, for myself and for other people?

- What objectives would I like to set myself on the basis of this exercise?

Who we are produces what we do — in love, social activities, family

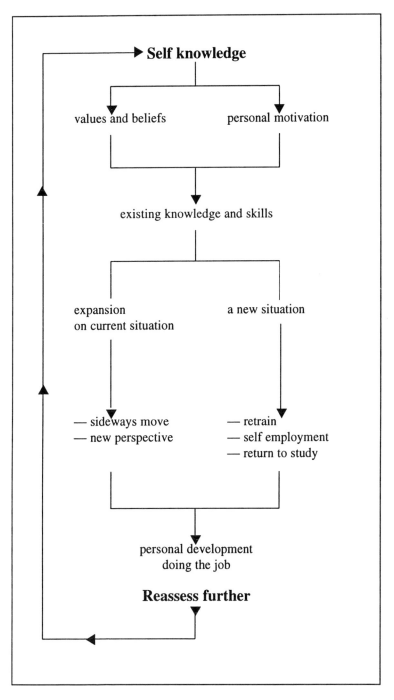

Fig. 8. Know thyself and get a better job.

relationships, hobbies and work. As we build a solid foundation of self discovery, we can erect a building that truly represents our inner self.

The face of work is changing. One piece of technology can do the work of several people. Certain industries have fallen, not to rise again. However, new industries have arisen and they need to be serviced — but not everyone is suited to everything.

Re-defining value systems helps to restructure the beliefs which fuel our motivation for work. As we evolve in our own life, so society evolves through its life. As we discover why we want to work and what we want to do, we can then start networking out into the community. We can begin the exciting journey of discovering how we can help each other achieve our goals.

CASE STUDIES

Angela needs to feel useful

Angela wants to be of use in her work. She has strong feelings about the community and society, especially women's issues. She is resourceful, independent, competent and resilient. Her work skills cover administration, finance, budgeting and organisation.

Studying for a Degree
How to succeed as a mature student in higher education
Stephen Wade

If you are an aspiring student in adult education, or a mature learner looking for a higher education course leading to a degree, this book is specially for you. It will lead you through the academic maze of entry procedures, study programmes and teaching methods. It explains how to apply and how to contact the professionals who will help; how to survive tutorials, seminars and presentations, and how to manage your time, plan your study, and find the right support when you need it. There are sections on the credit award system, pathway planning, and useful case studies of typical students in this context. Stephen Wade PhD has 20 years' professional experience in further and higher education, and is a Course Leader for a degree programme.

£8.99, 128pp illus. paperback. 1 85703 415 5.

Available from How To Books Ltd, Plymbridge House, Estover Road, Plymouth PL6 7PZ. Customer Services tel: (01752) 202301. Fax: (01752) 202331.

Please add postage & packing (£1 UK, £2 Europe, £3 world airmail).

Credit card orders may be faxed or phoned.

Robert needs a regular income
Robert has always wanted to be a printer ever since leaving school. He loves his work and having a productive and creative outlet makes him feel useful. He misses the male companionship. Having a regular income with the chance of overtime is one of his primary issues.

Alan needs status
Alan works for status, money and achievement. He enjoys the perks of his career and thrives on pressure and competitiveness. He is a very pro-active person and feels lost without several projects happening at once.

DISCUSSION POINTS

1. What is the difference between work and career?

2. What are the benefits of linking personal development to work?

3. How far should personal needs and motivations be expressed through work?

5
Setting up a Career Development Strategy

RESEARCHING THE JOB MARKET

Economic and labour trends

It is useful to consider the economic trends both nationally and locally when researching the job market. Issues such as the recession and the impact of local and national government budgets within your area may affect the economic flow and therefore your employment. Your local Chamber of Commerce, the Town Hall and Jobcentres could provide the information you require.

It is of benefit to you to research employment statistics within your locality. Do you live in a high unemployment area? Would it be worth widening your catchment area and commuting? Are there times of the year when there are more jobs on the market — before Christmas or during the summer? A temporary job during these times could lead to networking contacts.

Did you know:

- in general, employment amongst both full-time and part-time workers has increased

- those in part-time work now number about a quarter of all those in employment

- over the past two years, there has also been an increase in self employment

- the majority of full-time workers are men

- just under half of all women in employment are part-timers

- long-term claimant unemployment is falling

- in general, notified vacancies are increasing

- the most hard-to-fill vacancies are occurring in sales, personal and protective services and clerical/secretarial?

Keeping up to date with trends in technology

Although technology has enabled new markets and better service, it has also contributed to higher unemployment. Technology has, in part, replaced people. What happens to the people? They can learn either the skills to operate the technology or new skills. Applied technology is a booming market — computers, media, robotics, virtual reality — all steadily growing areas. If you choose to jump on the bandwagon and secure your future, you need to be aware of the development of technology in your field of expertise. Will employment dwindle as technology entrenches itself further? Do you want to be involved in that technology? Could you find a sideways niche in your market that doesn't involve so much technology? You need to keep up-to-date with developments and training opportunities. Or maybe you will decide to change your field of expertise altogether.

Be aware of the development of individual companies

Which companies are making people redundant in your area? What new companies are moving in? Are any established companies considering expansion?

Know the demand rate within your own professional area

Are you aware of the demand rate for your area of expertise? Is your work seasonal, *eg* lecturing? Do you need to upgrade your skills to keep abreast of current trends? Are you aware of new trends within your profession?

Do you know?

1. Which are the ten biggest factories in your county?

2. Which are the two biggest factories in your town?

3. Which are the ten biggest office firms in your county?

4. Which are the two biggest office firms in your town?

5. Which firms have announced redundancies in your town within the last six months?

6. Which new firms have moved into your town within the last six months?

RETURNING TO STUDY

As you do your research, it may become apparent that returning to study or re-training may be appropriate. Issues to consider might include:

- whether you want to return full or part-time

- costs such as course fees, exam fees, books and equipment, travel and childcare

- whether you want a confidence building course to prepare you for paid work

- whether you want a qualification course for a new job

- whether you want a course for updating skills in your current profession

- whether you want a course to help you set up in self employment

- what effects retraining might have on your benefits.

ORGANISING YOUR JOBSEARCH STRATEGY

Setting your target job
You will need to decide:

- what skills you want to use
- at what level you want to work
- in what market you want to work
- in what geographical area you want to work
- the salary you require.

Budgeting the cost of jobsearch
Your budget should include a financial allowance for the following:

- computer usage including paper, envelopes and printer cartridge
- stationery including stapler, paper clips and presentation folder
- subscriptions to periodicals, trade journals and newspapers
- reference books and manuals
- photocopying
- telephone
- car, including parking and petrol
- other travel
- postage.

Using Employment Services
Employment Services (ES) is part of the Civil Service arm and is the country's largest employment organisation. ES runs Jobcentres which can be found in almost every town. You will have a Client Adviser who can assist with:

(a) places on free courses for those returning to work or seeking to upgrade their jobsearch skills

(b) costs of travelling to interviews

(c) membership of jobclubs for networking, support and access to stationery

(d) direct access to jobs

(e) opportunities for you to try out jobs before committing yourself

(f) benefit advice and rebates.

When you make your first appointment to go to a Jobcentre, you will need to take your P45, your National Insurance number and your partner's National Insurance number if you wish to claim for an adult dependant.

Using the TECs
The Training and Enterprise Councils provide funding and access to a broad range of programmes including:

- career guidance

- Training for Work (helping the unemployed find jobs and achieve qualifications)

- Learning for Work (helping the unemployed to pursue full-time vocational studies).

Career counselling
This is a growing area of business where you will be charged for the service provided. There are both general and specific areas of counselling, *eg* women, redundancy, coming up to retirement. Career counselling:

- tells you about working environments
- may suggest possible contacts
- tells you what kind of jobs match your skills, needs and experience
- defines what skills are needed for a particular job
- recommends additional training to give credibility
- may uncover areas of employment you hadn't considered
- will challenge you to think more creatively.

Using registers and placement agencies
In general, these tend to cater for junior, professional and lower management. Some agencies cater for more specific requirements such as accountancy, secretarial and clerical, nurses or sales personnel. Charges are made to the employer and not to yourself. Be aware of being asked for money in return for work. This is unethical. Keep a record of the contacts you make with agencies (see Figure 9).

Colleges and universities
Colleges and universities have their own career counselling departments

---

MY AGENCY APPROACH CARD
Agency:
Telephone:
Contact Name:
Meeting:
Notes:

Fig. 9. Recording your agency contacts.

which outsiders may be able to access. They may also provide information on local employment opportunities.

Using the careers office
There are career centres in most large towns and they provide information on local employment opportunities, career descriptions, information on what skills are needed for a particular job, information on training and educational opportunities. They are primarily aimed at younger people.

Using the library
The reference part of any library is an invaluable source of information. They usually have the national and local papers for reference as well as trade directories for researching company profiles. You can access contact names, addresses and telephone numbers. A photocopier is usually available.

Opportunities through computer aided guidance
Jobcentres and libraries have computer aided guidance for TAPS (Training Access Points), giving information about training both locally and nationally.

Researching a prospective employer
You can access the latest accounts and other financial information plus directors' names from the Registrar of Companies and Limited Partnerships. Your local Chamber of Commerce may also be able to

---

MY COMPANY APPROACH CARD

Company:

Telephone:

Address:

Contact Name:

Position Applied For:

Research:

Interview:

Spec Letter:

Result:

Fig. 10. Recording your company contacts.

help. You can also use the company reference books in your local library.

MAKING SPECULATIVE CONTACTS

Direct mail could prove an effective way into a company. Selling yourself through a letter addressed to a decision-maker may bring in a lead or even an interview. Most employers respect initiative — and most vacancies are filled by the applicant being at the right place at the right time. Keep a record of your speculative approaches (see Figure 10).

USING THE MEDIA

Press advertisements

It isn't advisable to place an advertisement for your services unless you are self employed or looking to invest capital. Apart from the local press, professional and trade journals, the national newspapers are a good source of vacancies. Most concentrate on specific professional areas on particular days.

Setting up a Career Development Strategy

Appointment	Newspaper	Day
Art/communication	*Guardian*	Monday/Thursday
	Daily Telegraph	Monday
	Independent	Wednesday/Friday
	Daily Express	Tuesday
	Times	Wednesday
Teaching	*Daily Telegraph*	Thursday
	Guardian	Tuesday
	Independent	Thursday
	Daily Express	Tuesday/Thursday
	Times	Monday
Financial	*Daily Telegraph*	Monday
	Guardian	Thursday
	Independent	Tuesday
	Financial Times	Wednesday/Thursday
	Daily Mail	Wednesday
	Times	Thursday
Civil Service	*Daily Telegraph*	Monday
	Guardian	Wednesday/Friday
	Independent	Thursday
	Daily Mail	Wednesday
	Daily Express	Tuesday
	Times	Thursday
Information technology	*Daily Telegraph*	Monday
	Guardian	Thursday
	Independent	Monday
	Daily Mail	Thursday
	Daily Express	Thursday
	Times	Tuesday
Engineers	*Daily Telegraph*	Tuesday/Thursday
	Guardian	Thursday
	Independent	Monday
	Daily Mail	Thursday
	Daily Express	Monday/Tuesday
	Times	Thursday
Secretarial	*Daily Mail*	Tuesday
	Daily Express	Tuesday
	Times	Monday/Tuesday/Wednesday

Management	*Daily Telegraph*	Tuesday/Thursday/Saturday
	Guardian	Monday/Wednesday/Thursday
	Independent	Thursday/Sunday
	Financial Times	Wednesday
	Daily Mail	Thursday
	Daily Express	Monday/Wednesday/Thursday
	Times	Thursday
Science	*Daily Telegraph*	Monday/Thursday
	Guardian	Thursday
	Independent	Monday
	Daily Mail	Thursday
	Daily Express	Thursday
	Times	Thursday
Sales and marketing	*Daily Telegraph*	Wednesday/Thursday
	Guardian	Monday/Thursday
	Independent	Wednesday
	Financial Times	Wednesday
	Daily Mail	Tuesday/Thursday
	Daily Express	Wednesday
	Times	Thursday
Works management	*Daily Telegraph*	Thursday
	Guardian	Monday
	Independent	Monday/Thursday
	Daily Mail	Thursday
	Daily Express	Thursday
	Times	Thursday

STARTING TO NETWORK

What is networking?

Effective networking helps us to keep our balance and perspective. The right information, the best resources and the strongest support are needed to keep us focused in the midst of change.

Newspapers and journals I need to look at:		
	title	publication day/month
Relevant national papers:		
Local papers: town — county — Trade journals:		

Fig. 11. Using the media.

Why network?

- to make a career change
- to increase knowledge and expertise in your field of work
- to have your skills and expertise more visible to others.

Questions for assessing your networking needs

- What are my career goals for the next six months?
- What are my career goals for the next twelve months?
- Why are these goals important to me?
- Who can I get to help me achieve these goals?
- How can they help me achieve these goals?
- How will I know when I have achieved them?

How to network

- never ask for a job — ask for information
- keep in touch with your contact
- ask if you can do anything in return

- respect the limits of confidentiality
- be as active as you can in any institutions or clubs you belong to
- be assertive
- ask the right questions
- use effective image and presentation skills
- be viewed as knowledgeable or skilful
- network by telephone
- attend meetings and conferences
- write letters
- when approaching companies with spec letters locate the decision maker and make it clear you will be following up your inquiry.

Networking works in partnership by

- listening
- encouraging
- teaching
- sharing
- promoting
- challenging
- inspiring

Using personal contacts

You could use:

neighbours	social contacts
relatives	friends
doctor/dentist/optician	club contacts
local shopkeepers	vet
past college friends	past university friends
old boy/girl network	priest/rabbi/minister
rotary clubs colleagues	Freemasons

Using professional contacts

You could use:

previous clients	former work contacts
tutors	consultants
professional organisations	customers
suppliers	solicitors
fellow members of professional associations	accountants

Setting up a Career Development Strategy 71

past employers
veterans associations
meetings and conferences
new names from trade journal/company brochures/newspapers/magazines

military organisations
voluntary institutions

Starting a formal network

It might be possible to start a formal network after being told of your redundancy but before you leave. Or you could initiate a network after leaving. The methods you could use might include:

- newsletters
- brochures
- speeches
- staff meetings
- being a floater
- getting a mentor
- building a team by sponsoring or mentoring others
- getting sponsors
- networking your boss
- doing favours — bank some favours
- continually maintaining visibility through teaching, writing, speaking and leading.

You can keep a record of your networking contacts in the same way as for agencies and speculative approaches to companies.

Your support network

A support network is made up of personal contacts (not including professionals) who can support you as you redefine, change and grow through this phase of career development.

My support network needs to include

- someone I can rely upon in a crisis
- someone whom I can talk to when I am worried
- someone who mentally stimulates me
- someone I can have fun with socially
- someone whom I can feel close to
- someone who values me
- someone who challenges me
- someone who gives me constructive feedback.

CREATING YOUR OWN JOB

You might feel as you do your research, both on yourself and on the market trends, that there is no job for you out there. In which case, create your own and become self employed.

So you've done your research and you are considering whether to return to study or organise your jobsearch strategy. Whatever you choose, it should reflect how you think and feel at this point. Everything is open to change and you may find your decisions now aren't appropriate in six months' time. You may find problems along the way and you will need perseverance and lateral thinking to overcome them.

CASE STUDIES

Angela networks

Using her contacts built up as a personal assistant, Angela was aware that redundancy was in the air long before any formal announcement came. Consequently, she used the opportunity to get onto as many in-house training courses as possible to begin networking. She realised that insurance and financial management services were potential growth areas and that there were gaps in the market for small but competitive companies. After she left, she worked on consolidating relationships with freelance financial managers whom she had networked with on courses when employed.

Robert learns new skills

Robert realised the print industry was gradually being taken over by modern technology and the traditional methods of printing were slowly becoming obsolete. Unwillingly, he accepted that he would have to be receptive to learning new technology as part of his job strategy. The print trade is usually very much linked to economic trends. If there is a recession or companies are in financial difficulty, printed matter is usually the first to be stopped. Printing jobs are usually advertised in the union magazine, but more vacancies are filled through word of mouth than by adverts.

Alan looks at self-employment

Before being made redundant, Alan was feeling squeezed by the recession and was beginning to consider changing his career focus. He was also beginning to realise how much of his stress was due to the uncer-

Setting up a Career Development Strategy

tainty of his job security. He was considering self-employment, feeling he could create his own work and be more in control.

DISCUSSION POINTS

1. What benefits are there in the new age of technology?

2. Consider why the majority of vacancies are not advertised.

3. How can you make yourself part of another network?

6
Overcoming Barriers

WHAT ARE BARRIERS?

When we have had a hard knock in life, it can take our confidence away. Being told we are no longer required for work can arouse unwelcome feelings and thoughts. We can often slip into a victim role where we believe that our misfortunes are due to the Government, God, the local council, our age or health or anything else. The barriers we perceive may be very real or we may have a subconscious need to make a barrier real in order to compensate for a lack of self-esteem. It can sometimes be easier to blame a barrier than to take responsibility for ourselves. There is no doubt that genuine difficulties do sometimes exist when trying to get back to work. But with some positive thought, a common sense approach and perseverance, we can overcome most of the constraints.

Sexism
Sex discrimination
The Equal Opportunities Commission will assist if you need help or advice on sexual harassment, sex discrimination or equal pay.

Gays and lesbians
If you are experiencing work problems related to your sexuality, Lesbian and Gay Employment Rights can give advice, support and information.

Ageism
When we look for new employment, we may find that we are either too young or too old for a job. Sometimes it may seem as if there is no employment for our particular age group. Some jobs require youth, others require employees at a peak of around 35 and then there is the widening market for the more mature person.

Overcoming Barriers

Some of the benefits of maturity include:

- commitment
- life experience
- increased confidence
- proven skills
- fewer family distractions
- company loyalty
- reliability
- stability
- tolerance

Salaried work

Areas such as management, court work, housekeeping, retail, financial services, tutoring and counselling all benefit from maturity. Jobs such as being a driving instructor, a beauty therapist or a careers adviser also appeal to people of a more mature age.

> **There is an employment market for all age groups if you look in the right places**

Hints for the mature person's CV

- concentrate on your relevant strengths of character

- emphasise your skills and experience

- omit dates on your educational/qualification information

- put a personal profile after your name on the CV

- put your most relevant/recent work experience after your name on the CV

- place personal details without a date of birth at the end (unless asked for)

- mention additional information such as special skills, languages, current courses, computer literacy

- indicate physical and mental fitness and agility

- indicate an up-to-date and motivated attitude.

Self employment
Working for yourself later in life has its advantages. It can be the chance to try a different career which unlocks your hidden talents. You could use your experience to set up as a consultant, buy into an existing business or franchise or start making money from a hobby.

Overcoming literacy/numeracy problems
Literacy and numeracy problems can have a variety of sources: a scattered early education, language difficulties, family problems in childhood or dyslexia. When there are difficulties with reading, writing or maths, this can undermine confidence and raise feelings of frustration, shame and anger. Those who are in this position may feel stupid when in fact this is not the case. Dyslexia especially can give rise to misplaced labels of not being intelligent. Help is available to anyone, individually and in small groups. There are free classes in every town to cater for those with literacy and numeracy problems. There is specific help for those suffering from dyslexia.

Dependants
It may be that your role as parent or carer is holding you back from retraining or applying for jobs. Flexible jobsearch solutions may include:

- self employment
- tele-working from home
- job-sharing
- term-time working.

Possible study/retraining solutions could include:

- open learning
- distance learning
- the Open University.

Location and travel

Relocation
Relocation may be offered as an alternative to redundancy or it may offer the opportunity for a new job in a better employment area. Companies' information may include; financial and housing matters, schooling information and spouse employment assistance.

Transport
It may be that there are plenty of jobs within your specification but outside your area and you don't have your own transport or you don't drive. The possible options here could be to:

- take out a loan for transport
- learn to drive
- take public transport
- find someone who works near you or with you and share the petrol costs.

If you have an interview away from home, you may be able to get help to pay the cost of travelling including unavoidable overnight stays. Check with your local Jobcentre for details of the Travel to Interview Scheme.

Overcoming a criminal record

If you are an ex-prisoner, it might serve you better at this stage to get into education or training. NACRO may be able to help.

Overcoming lack of experience or skills

Adult education
Your local adult education college could provide a way to brush up on old (or new) skills.

Further education
The local colleges offer qualification courses to both young and mature students. You could study part-time without affecting benefits or you could become a full-time student with a grant.

Jobskills
There are various government schemes (which you can find out about at your local Jobcentre) which offer skills training with and without qualifications. You are also supported in your jobsearch while learning and you can still claim benefits.

Voluntary work
Visiting your local volunteer bureau could increase your feelings of usefulness plus provide excellent material for your CV. It will also provide references, increase your skills base, expose you to different working envi-

ronments, increase your confidence and provide networking opportunities.

Community Action
This service provided by your local Jobcentre is a useful way back into employment. The projects are geared specifically towards the community or the environment. During the time you are involved, you continue to receive benefit plus an additional £10 per week and jobsearch advice and assistance.

The benefit loop
Sometimes employment doesn't offer much more financial reward than if you stayed on benefits. Family Credit is one option which could increase your salary.

The economic climate
Financial wizards and politicians are always telling us we're on our way into or out of a recession. Someone once told me 'this too will pass'. At that time I was down, so these words of wisdom cheered me up. However, when I was happy and I remembered her words — I didn't feel so good. At the end of the day, we are each in charge of our own destiny. Of course we can be affected by outside circumstances, but we can either go up or down with them or we can make our own luck. Don't be seduced by the media telling you that there is no money out there — no jobs — and all is doom and gloom. Don't fall into self-fulfilling prophecies. Understand that all you need is one job and that there will always be room for you as a conscientious employed person. Unemployment has nothing to do with you — don't let other people's negativity empty your hopes.

Health

Disability Employment Adviser
The Disability Employment Adviser (DEA) at your Jobcentre can help you make the most of your abilities. They can also assist with getting equipment to help you in your work. The DEA is part of the Placing, Assessment and Counselling Team (PACT). There is an Access to Work scheme available which can provide help up to the value of £21,000 over five years.

Ethnic origin
The Commission for Racial Equality may be able to assist you if you are being harassed.

Overcoming job competition

Selling yourself
You are your own sales representative and your marketing tools should include:

- the CV
- skill in completing application forms
- letter writing skills (for covering and spec letters)
- finding the market need
- surviving selection tests
- handling interviews (and interviewers)
- networking
- telephone techniques.

Creating a need
Find the need in the market and you could be in with a chance. If you don't immediately see the job of your life being offered in the local paper, approach companies on spec and sell yourself. If you sell yourself well enough, you may make a prospective employer want to see you even if there apparently isn't a job there. If you really are good enough, they will employ you because your main sales pitch is aimed at creating a need in them for your skills and experience (even though they didn't realise they needed them in the first place).

Making your own job
If the ideal job isn't there, if you can't create a need in a prospective employer, then create a niche in the market completely for yourself and become self employed.

Job Search Seminar
Your local Jobcentre can arrange for you to attend a Job Search Seminar which will assist you with interview techniques, CV preparation and other practical details of applying for work, thereby increasing your chances of returning to work.

Job Interview Guarantee
Another service from the Jobcentre is the JIG scheme — Job Interview Guarantee. As part of the register, your skills and qualifications are matched quickly against employers' vacancies as soon as they are received.

Need for a high income
In the heady days of the eighties when jobs were plentiful and money flowed, many people built up a lifestyle to go with it all. Come the nineties and the job market fluctuation, money now comes in dribs and drabs — but the lifestyle has been committed to. Re-organising your lifestyle and financial structure is really the only way of dealing with this problem. There is also an abundance of lower paid jobs which doesn't help to solve the problem. Family Credit may help to raise a low salary but not necessarily the lifestyle.

'No one replies to my CV/application'
When you apply for a job, you may be one of 20 or 30 applicants. When you are rejected, it is your skills and experience that aren't suitable — **not you personally**. Try again and again and again. As long as you have CVs and application forms out in circulation, there is hope.

Been out of work too long
Your CV
When you write your CV, make sure that you can write truthfully 'unemployed but doing voluntary work' or 'unemployed but attending a word processing course'. Show that you have been filling in your time productively.

Voluntary work
Doing voluntary work could serve several purposes:

- something constructive to put on your CV
- taking your mind off your own problems
- the opportunity to try different environments
- developing new skills
- networking opportunities

BUILDING UP SHATTERED CONFIDENCE

What is confidence?

- taking pride in who we are and what we do while allowing others that same privilege

- the knowledge that whatever we think and feel has validity

- respecting our right for self expression while respecting the rights of others

- becoming powerful

- developing power and control over ourselves and communicating this in an assertive manner while respecting the rights of others to do the same

- believing in who we are.

What helps us to become confident?
Trusting others
Safe people listen and hear you. They make eye contact and accept the real you. They are non-judgemental, direct, supportive and loyal. At our deepest levels, we know what is best and right for us. Ultimately, we need to trust ourselves. Others can advise us, but only we can have the final responsibility.

Positive interaction
We need to learn good communication skills in order to relate fully and openly with others. When we can learn to disclose appropriately and are able to listen to the disclosures of others, we can share, support and be supported.

Listening to others as they feedback their observations of our behaviour is a vital tool to self discovery. We can share our thoughts and feelings without giving away our personal power and we can also learn from others.

Most of us find criticism from others hard to take. We don't like to think we are not perfect. Ironically, we know we are not perfect: we worry over not being right, but at the same time we fear being criticised. We interpret criticism as an attack on our very personal self. In truth, constructive criticism is an observation on our behaviour — not our entire way of being. The observation may be accurate or it may not be.

When giving criticism, we need to be sure of being objective and rational. When receiving criticism, we can choose to accept or reject the criticism. We need to learn to lovingly criticise ourselves, to give constructive criticism to others, to reject inappropriate criticism and take constructive criticism from others.

Appropriate action and positive life experiences
As our confidence grows and we learn to trust our own judgement more, we are able to take decisive action. It may not always be the right action, but we feel confident enough to be able to take further action to handle mistakes.

Being confident doesn't mean we no longer experience negative emotions. The difference with increased self esteem is that we have the awareness to recognise how we feel and we have developed the skills to deal with them appropriately. Self expression means balancing the polarities of negative and positive. We cannot have one without the other. The more we numb the negative, the more we numb the positive. However, with increased confidence, we are able to feel through the entire spectrum, thereby making us a whole person.

When we are open, receptive and in control, we can fulfil our hopes and dreams. Life isn't limited and boring. It becomes unlimited and exciting, bound only by our imagination.

BREAKING DOWN EXPECTATIONS

Of others
We should work in order to satisfy ourselves, but often we work to satisfy the needs and expectations of others. Our mother might have always wanted us to be a nurse, a spouse might enjoy having a high-flying partner, our father might want us to follow in the family business. If we have tended to go into jobs to satisfy others, we may subconsciously sabotage our work situation through blaming others or resentment. Consequently, if we find ourselves out of work, we may not be very motivated to find new employment.

Of ourselves
We may have expectations of ourselves. Maybe we were told how brilliant we were when younger, when actually we weren't. Maybe we were told how stupid we were, when actually we weren't. We may believe that we couldn't learn or achieve anything.

LOOKING AT OUR VALUES

It is possible that our value system gets in the way of us getting satisfactory employment. We may have political beliefs which could cause resentment about the haves and have-nots. We may feel guilty about earning money which causes conflict. We may hate authority which causes problems working for others. We may want to do work which benefits the community but doesn't pay enough for the mortgage.

Overcoming constraints forces us to examine our thoughts and beliefs. It is only natural when we come to employment hurdles to hesitate, but in the long run we can do no good by allowing constraints to overcome us. We must find ways of overcoming them. Sometimes we may have to accept that we cannot overcome them at this precise moment. Maybe we will have to compromise. But armed with knowledge, foresight and determination, we can find a way through to a new way of working.

CASE STUDIES

Angela plays the maturity card
Angela is in her 40s and faces stiff competition from younger, more skilled administrators. But she realises her maturity and experience can work for her if she considers becoming self employed in financial management. As she is considering working in partnership with a male colleague, the fact of her being a woman could also be an advantage with potential clients. Using her networking contacts, she is also able to update skills by attending courses.

Robert gains confidence
Robert doesn't drive and so location of potential work could be a problem. Although he lives by a railway station, he would consider buying a bicycle if necessary. His main constraint is a lack of con-fidence which he is learning to handle by talking over his fears with his wife.

Alan re-examines his needs
Alan is aware that his age is against him if he is to search for employment. He is also beginning to realise just how driven he is. His father had been a lawyer and had encouraged his son to achieve status through money. When Alan married, his wife didn't work but had expensive tastes which re-inforced his need for a high salary. He is now beginning to understand that he too has his needs and the enforced respite due to redundancy, is encouraging him to rethink his values.

DISCUSSION POINTS

1. How can competitiveness for jobs improve your attitude towards your work?

2. Is it possible for a person of the opposite gender to yourself to do the kind of work you do as well as yourself?

3. How can maturity benefit the kind of work you are at present searching for?

7
Choosing a Mode of Work

The working day of nine till five, five days a week until you retire is going. As the larger social order changes and economic trends fluctuate, this is reflected in new and evolving modes of work. Did you know:

- flexible employment is now essential

- few employers predict a return to traditional patterns of full-time core employment

- contracting out is likely to occur in facilities such as management, driving and distribution and data preparation

- there is a substantial increase in part-time work and job sharing.

CHOOSING INTERIM MANAGEMENT

Due to cutbacks, some firms are reluctant to take on extra permanent staff. As a consequence, a new service has emerged which supplies temporary executive or interim managers. Fees can range, according to your skills and experience, from £150 - £300 daily.

CHOOSING TERM-TIME WORKING

When a company has a policy of encouraging women returners, they may introduce a scheme called Term-Time Working. This scheme offers a contract for a limited number of weeks per year plus the same conditions of work as full-timers including sick pay and training opportunities. There is usually a stipulation that holidays must be taken during school holidays with the right to additional unpaid leave during school holidays.

CHOOSING TO WORK FROM HOME

It is possible to have a regular job, get paid for it and stay at home to do it. Many large companies operate tele-working schemes whereby employees use information technology and telecommunications from home.

BUYING A FRANCHISE

A franchise is the authorisation to sell a company's goods or services in a particular area. Some pointers to bear in mind:

- make your own choice of advisers, *eg* solicitor and accountant
- talk to existing franchisees
- look at arrangements for purchasing equipment and stock
- examine what happens if you want to renew or sell your franchise
- investigate the franchiser
- make sure the franchiser belongs to the British Franchise Association
- check that you have exclusive rights to sell within the territory allocated
- carry out market research in the same way as if you were setting up in business on your own
- find out how advertising levels will be maintained.

BEING A PORTFOLIO PERSON

Because of new ways to work, a new label has sprung up. The Portfolio Person is someone who has two or three jobs. I'm a portfolio person — I am a manager/trainer delivering Employment Service programmes and commercial training, a writer on career and life management and a professional astrologer.

CHOOSING TEMPORARY WORK

Temporary work covers almost any sphere of employment and could provide an opportunity to try out different working environments and companies. It is also a good way to network and you might even find more permanent work coming out of it.

CHOOSING FLEXI-TIME

If you choose this mode of work, it gives you greater control over your time. You would be paid for a set number of hours each week or month. Usually there is a set time where you will have to be at work, but there would also be a flexible time period at the beginning and end of the day where you could fit in your flexible hours. You could gain by having time for children, medical visits, holidays or shopping. One of the attractive elements of this scheme is that a certain amount of hours can be built up for annual leave. Another perk is that travelling is easier and cheaper outside peak times. Routine office and administrative work is most suitable to this way of working.

CHOOSING TO JOBSHARE

Jobshare is normally applicable to a full time position and introduces part-time hours. Two people share the same job, dividing the hours and responsibilities between them. Senior and managerial levels in particular are benefiting from this way of working. Another benefit may be to provide career and work opportunities for carers and those who are disabled.

CHOOSING CONTRACT WORK

This type of work is becoming more commonplace. A contract differs from temporary work in that it is usually longer term with more benefits.

CHOOSING PART-TIME WORK

According to government definition, a part-timer is someone who works less than 30 hours per week. Technically the fewer hours you work, the less favourably you may get treated. In general though, conditions for part-timers have improved over the past few years:

- those who work less than eight hours per week have limited rights

- those who work 16 or more hours per week and have been with the same employer for more than two years are entitled to redundancy pay, maternity pay and leave

- those who work less than 16 hours per week and have been with the same employer for more than five years are entitled to redundancy pay, maternity pay and leave

Part-time work is an ideal way to combine working with caring.

CHOOSING TO WORK ABROAD

Members of the European Union (EU) have the right to live and work in other member states (Belgium, Denmark, Republic of Ireland, France, Germany, Greece, Italy, Luxembourg, Netherlands, Spain, Portugal and the UK) without a work permit. UK nationals working in another member state have the same rights as nationals of that country with regard to salary, working conditions, training, social security and housing.

The Overseas Placing Unit (OPU) is a division of the Employment Services and can be contacted at the Jobcentre. They have access to overseas vacancies held on the national vacancy system and the Oracle Jobfinder system. If you wish to find work outside the EU, the OPU can give advice, but there is no current system for exchange of applications between the UK and these countries. These vacancies will be handled by recruitment agencies.

CHOOSING TO BE SELF EMPLOYED

Being self employed is an option worth considering if you like to be in control, enjoy a challenge and have a good idea to fill a niche in the market-place. Some benefits include:

- achieving your full potential
- taking whatever risks you like
- working the hours you want
- improving your self confidence
- avoiding being unemployed
- working at something you enjoy
- making unlimited money
- learning about business.

Market research
There is no point in having a great idea if no one wants it. Market research is the foundation for any good business. Find out what the punters want and make sure you are the one to provide it.

Some questions for market research

1. Is your target market for consumers, industry or professionals?

2. If selling into a consumer market, what are the personal factors affecting the purchasers of your product or service — their interests, income, age, marital status, social class, family size, gender?

3. What are the purchaser's reasons for buying the product or service?

4. Is your potential market likely to grow in the future?

5. How do the potential customers/clients buy — shop, mail order etc?

6. Who are your competitors (names, strengths and weaknesses, product or service, prices)? How well have they done in the last few years? How is the company organised? How do they produce their goods? Who are their main customers/clients? How do they market their product or service?

Business skills
Having the best idea since sliced bread and knowing you have a desperate market waiting to give you their money is only half the battle. The other 50% is using your business skills so that you can administer and develop your business successfully.

Raising capital
You could start up a business with part or all of your redundancy money. Alternative sources might include:

- banks
- private loans (be aware of loan sharks)
- money from local authorities
- Government initiatives
- money through the EU
- overdraft facilities

Have you had experience of: *Circle*

- keeping accounting books — Yes No Some
- debt chasing — Yes No Some
- installing a system of credit control — Yes No Some
- negotiating credit terms — Yes No Some
- drawing up cash flows — Yes No Some
- cash control — Yes No Some
- drawing up budgets — Yes No Some
- estimating/raising long-term financial need — Yes No Some
- drawing up business plans — Yes No Some
- presenting your plan to financiers — Yes No Some
- establishing prices — Yes No Some
- sales — Yes No Some
- market sector analysis — Yes No Some
- advertising — Yes No Some
- public relations — Yes No Some
- product distribution — Yes No Some
- stock control — Yes No Some
- recruiting staff — Yes No Some
- project management — Yes No Some
- management team building — Yes No Some

Fig. 12. Your business skills assessment.

Choosing a Mode of Work

- option of leasing or hire purchase as an alternative to raising a lump sum
- if your need for cash is related to difficulties with credit control, consider invoice factoring
- consider turning personal assets into cash
- approach a merchant bank or private individual for venture capital.

Costings

As part of your costings and organisational strategy, you will need to consider:

- telephone
- computers
- printing
- advertising
- furniture
- premises
- production
- materials
- vehicles
- your salary
- employing others

Your business identity

Your business identity refers to how you will trade — on your own or with others:

1. sole trader
2. a partnership
3. a limited company

Marketing

Without a marketing campaign, you have no sales. The way in which you sell is your marketing campaign. Ways of getting your message across to the public include:

posters	ads	sales letters
letterbox drops	press releases	direct mail
radio	TV	public speaking
leaflets	brochures	seminars
forums	sponsorships	agents
writing articles	writing books	hoardings

Ask yourself:

- What is my product or service?
- What is the selling price and cost of my product or service?
- What sort of marketing will I do?
- Who will do the selling?
- What is my sales pitch?

Selling skills

You have had the idea, researched the potential, produced the goods — now you have to tell everyone about it.

Know	— the main features of your product or service
	— the major benefits it offers
	— the most likely objections and your planned response
	— the advantages and weaknesses of competitors
	— key characteristics of your potential buyer
	— in what ways your product or service meets the buyers' needs and wants
Listen	— to your buyer
Relate	— what you are selling to your buyers' needs and wants
Plan	— your strategy for each prospective buyer
	— your sales presentations, telephone calls or demonstrations
Make sure	— you know who the decision-maker is.

The law and you

Knowing the law and its relevance to your business gives security and credibility. You will need to:

- obtain professional advice from solicitor and accountant
- choose a legal form of business identity for your business
- comply with business or company name regulations
- register for VAT
- notify the Inland Revenue and the DSS of your business status
- consider your need for patents, copyright or trade mark registration
- comply with the laws affecting business premises and trading
- consider the need for a licence
- know your rights as an employer
- know your insurance needs
- pay the business rate.

Professional back-up

Behind every successful business person is a team of professionals, including:

- the accountant
- the bank
- the solicitor
- the surveyor/estate agent
- the designer
- the corporate financial adviser

Checklist for business failure

- overestimating sales
- underpricing
- lack of marketing skills
- failing to adapt your product or service to meet buyer's needs
- lack of skills in financial matters
- boredom
- fear.

Checklist for business success

- financing is sufficient to cover the shortfall of working capital especially in the early days
- the idea and market have potential growth
- diversification
- finger on current trends
- motivation
- confidence
- flexibility
- the will to succeed.

CASE STUDIES

Angela thinks about partnership

Angela is considering self employment, but working in partnership with someone else. Among other advantages, this could allow her to take time off without having to close the business.

Robert faces unsocial hours

Robert's trade works on a contractual basis. However, the hours of work

WHAT MODE SUITS YOU?

Term-time working	Do I mind long holidays with the children?
Working from home	Am I disciplined? Am I organised? Do I like working alone? Do I like being at home all the time?
Temporary work	Do I want to be constantly changing job? Can I make friends easily? Am I adaptable?
Flexi-time	Would I make use of the flexi-time?
Jobshare	Do I like to share? How do I feel about someone else taking over my work when I'm not there? Can I negotiate and compromise?
Contract work	Do I mind being given a remit to fulfil?
Self employment	Do I mind giving up a regular income? Do I want to borrow money? Can I work on my own? Can I live with insecurity about income? Do I mind working unsociable hours? Do I want to sell to strangers?
The portfolio person	Do I like the idea of having two or three different jobs? Am I multi-skilled?

Choosing a Mode of Work

are unsociable. They might either be early shift one week (6am-2pm) and late the next (2-10pm) or a continental shift which necessitates working six days for twelve hours a day with the next six days off.

Alan assembles a portfolio
Alan is considering becoming a portfolio person, working as a self employed consultant with occasional lecturing and writing.

DISCUSSION POINTS

1. What could be the benefits to you of being a portfolio person?

2. What changes have there been in your particular profession regarding the modes of work available?

3. Explore the possible social and economic reasons for the changes in the way we work.

8
Selling Yourself

When our fridge-freezer finally dies a death, we identify a need for a replacement. So we shop around for something which fulfils that need, looks good and is reliable. Metaphorically, you are that fridge-freezer. You have certain skills, knowledge and experience which you want to sell. Either you can wait for someone to come along and buy you — trusting that you will have what they want — or you can be constantly improving and updating what you have to offer. But employment is not only about **what** you offer but **how** you offer it. Your sales pitch, communication style and presentation will entice the buyer to look at what you're offering more closely.

COMMUNICATING IN DIFFERENT WAYS

Communication styles

Informing:	to impart information
Directing:	to guide other people's behaviour
Confrontational:	to challenge other people's automatism
Supporting:	to affirm other people's worth
Releasing:	to help other people to deal with emotions
Catalytic:	to provoke self discovery in other people.

Body language
Willing to listen and be friendly

sitting forward	nodding
direct eye contact	asking questions
interjecting with supportive comments	using non-threatening gestures
initiating and maintaining conversation	using a little humour in speech
being polite and courteous	smiling

sitting with unfolded
  arms and legs
reflective responding
even and deep breathing
a modulated, even
  voice tone

static body and posture
an upright body
head slightly on side
crinkled eyes

Anxious to interrupt
placing hand on arm
scowling
narrowed eyes
turning away
fidgeting

frowning
pursed lips
shallow breathing
gaze constantly shifting

Frustrated or rejected
scowling
narrow eyes
thumping hands together
  or hitting table top
raising tone of voice
white face
  (unpredictable anger)
a monotonic tone
using aggressive, downward
  hand gestures

frowning
pursed lips
tightening clothes

red face (explosive anger)
withdrawing from conversation

using one-syllable responses

Feeling threatened
folding arms or
  crossing legs
frowning
raised tone of voice

scowling

withdrawing eye contact
standing ground

Feeling superior
leaning back in chair
arms behind head
making sure body
  position is above others
grasping lapels of jacket
  and raising head
interrupting

legs over arm of chair
ignoring comments of others
looking at ceiling when talking

stabbing fingers

Not wishing to communicate
ignoring others looking down
erecting physical barrier
 to communication

Listening skills

We are not necessarily brought up to be good listeners. Most of us can hear as a purely physical function, but whether we actually listen to the content is another matter. We may be so full of our own thoughts and feelings, we block out what others are saying to us. Good listening skills involve:

- self discipline

- an openness to being challenged by others

- paying attention to verbal and non-verbal communication

- being able to keep confidences.

Using the right questions

Personal responsibility questions
You may be asked this type of question by the interviewer, 'How do you see your skills contributing to the effectiveness of this organisation?'

Elaboration questions
These questions give the other person a chance to expand on what they are talking about: for example, you may ask the interviewer, 'Could you tell me more about that part of the job?' or they may ask you 'Is there anything more you can tell me about your responsibilities in your last position?'

Speech

Speech patterns that let you down
excessive apologies   hedging, *eg* perhaps
disclaimers, *eg* I'm   fillers, *eg* well, y'know
 probably wrong but –
super polite speech   weak voice
excessive chit-chat   tag questions, *eg* aren't I right?
lengthy requests   too many questions
self-effacing remarks   wobbly or whining voice

sarcasm
speaking in a monotone
hesitancy
boastfulness
put downs
shoulds and oughts

shouting
too rapid
excessive 'I'
threatening questions
blame

Speech patterns that work
steady, even pace
sincere
controlled and fluent
emphasise key words
problem solving
constructive use of the 'I' word
using words like — let's, how can we resolve this?

clear
calm
making suggestions
brief and to the point
using questions
constructive criticism

Communication questionnaire

Imagine that you are the interviewer. Which of the mannerisms listed would encourage or discourage you to listen and respond favourably? Tick the positive and place a cross by the negative.

whispering
bouncing a leg
looking out of window
tugging ear
looking down
looking alert
occasionally smiling
offering a firm handshake

looking vacant
leaning far back
grinning
tapping fingers
direct eye contact
looking neat and clean
upright posture
chin stroking

picking nose
staring at you
shutting eyes
shuffling feet
looking anxious
covering the mouth
picking fluff
chewing nails

What verbal and non-verbal mannerisms do you have which might discourage others?

CREATING YOUR IMAGE AND STYLE

Whether you're male or female, wearing the colours and style which represent the real you makes you feel and look good and also has a powerful influence on those who see you. Did you know:

- 55% of your success depends upon visual factors
- 38% of your success depends upon your voice
- 7% of your success depends upon your spoken word
- **your success will happen within the first three minutes of entering the room.**

Colour

The colours you wear convey certain impressions to those you are with. Did you know:

- red says you are confident, energised, outgoing, agressive and authoritative

- white says you are detached, clinical and fresh

- green says you are dependable, security minded, calming, stubborn and self-reliant

- blue says you are trustworthy, clam, intuitive and confident

- magenta says you are gentle, kind and compassionate

- turquoise says you are approachable, youthful and clear

- pink says you are elegant, soothing and non-threatening

- black says you are powerful, traditional, formal and aloof

- violet says you are dignified and creative

- brown says you are safe, dedicated, materialistic, fixed and grounded

- yellow says you are successful, active, logical, controller, open minded, constructive and cheerful

- orange says you are enthusiastic, assertive, creative and energised

- grey says you are unapproachable and authoritarian

If you have a pink, beige, black or milky white complexion with blonde, brown, blue-grey, brunette, silvery-grey or white hair with blue, grey, hazel black or grey-green eyes, go for white, beige, blue-green, pinks, blue, red or green colours.

If you have an ivory, peachy pink, golden beige or black complexion with blonde, red, brown or golden grey hair with blue, green or brown eyes, go for ivory, beige, yellow-greens, light oranges and corals, reds, aquas and turquoise and browns.

Style

When going for an interview, it is vital that you convey the right visual impression. Styles of dress depend upon the environment you're going into. If you're going for a creative job, then your clothes need to reflect your individuality. If going for an executive position, classic suits may be called for. Your clothes should reflect the position, but they should also reflect the real you. Never wear anything you don't suit or don't feel at ease in. Whether male or female, you need to consider your body shape and height. Earrings are to a woman what a tie is to a man — they both draw attention to the face.

READING THE JOB ADVERTISEMENT

When replying to an advertisement for vacancies, you need to read the job description carefully for both the stated and hidden requirements. Take the following ad based on a real vacancy:

COWFIELD DAIRIES LTD

Cowfield Dairies is a progressive dairy with a production unit and 6 depots operating along the south-east coast and surrounding area.

We deliver to 50,000 customers each day, providing an excellent doorstep service for milk and other dairy products. We now require additional Roundspersons.

If you are looking for long-term security with an expanding organisation we would like to hear from you. If you are:

— a mature person
— physically fit
— living locally
— prepared to work week-ends
— prepared for an early start
— holder of a clean driving licence

FOR AN APPLICATION FORM
contact Martin Jones,
Cowfield Dairies Ltd, Norfolk.
Telephone 123456

Stated *(the obvious)*	**Hidden** *(the inferred)*
a mature person	someone who can grow along with a growing organisation
physically fit	
living locally	salesperson
prepared to work week-ends	good communication skills
prepared for an early start	good with money
holder of a clean driving licence	knows the area
looking for long term security	enjoys driving

When you apply for a job by telephone or letter, and in your interview, you should be armed with the qualities they want to buy from you. So by discovering the stated and hidden agenda in a job description, you are ready to supply your prospective employers with what they need.

Project

Take an ad from a newspaper or trade journal you would use in your job-search and work out the stated and hidden requirements.

USING THE TELEPHONE

When you telephone a company, either in response to an advert or on spec, your chances of selling yourself will depend on the character and enthusiasm coming across in your voice. Some proven tips include:

- having a clear idea of what you want from the call before dialling

- knowing the name and title of the person you want to speak to

- speaking in a lively and enthusiastic manner (smiling helps)

- speaking firmly and clearly

- don't suppress your body language (try standing up while on the phone if you want to feel more authoritative)

- listen with your right ear to absorb facts and your left ear for extra intuition

- listen to the tone and pitch of voice for hidden meaning.

Selling Yourself

Self assessment
What would you do if:

- the receptionist says 'I'm putting you through' and then you wait for ages with nothing happening?

- the name the receptionist has given you sounds like Mrs Snotsbody?

- when calling on spec, someone says 'The person in charge of recruitment is not around'.

Project
Speak into a tape recorder for five minutes, selling yourself to a prospective employer. What do you sound like?

CREATING YOUR CV

Tips
Your CV is your sales document — selling you to prospective employees:

- a CV should be no longer than two pages

- individually target each CV for the vacancy you are applying for

- have your CV word processed or typed

- don't use coloured paper.

Your CV format
The chronological CV
This is good for emphasising career growth and work experience, indicating a solid work history:

- start with your most recent position detailing the last four or five positions over the past ten years

- stress major accomplishments and responsibilities

- keep your target job in mind and emphasise prior positions which are relevant

- if you have completed a qualification course within the past five years put this at the top of your CV.

The functional CV
This is appropriate for an erratic work history and emphasises specific areas of skill:

- include four or five separate sections, each one detailing an area of expertise

- make the first section the one most relevant to the vacancy you are applying for

- within each section detail your accomplishments and abilities

- if you have completed a qualification course within the past five years put this at the top of your CV

- give a brief synopsis of your employment history at the bottom.

What to include in your CV

1. full name

2. if you haven't worked for some time, put your personal profile details at the top after your name

3. your full address and postcode

4. your telephone number and STD code

5. marital status

6. date of birth

7. your education (specifically secondary — exams passed)

8. further education (which college and when — exams/qualifications passed)

9. professional training (where and when — qualifications gained)

10. employment history (include work experience, placements, Saturday

jobs, holiday work; if there are gaps in your employment history put down the years rather than specific months; for gaps in employment put down something like 'unemployed but working in a voluntary capacity' or 'unemployed but took a course in learning German'; if you have a work history, begin with your most recent position — company, address, date from and to, responsibilities and achievements)

11. hobbies (making them relevant to the position you are seeking without bending the truth too much; add club membership or any positions of responsibility you have had as part of your interests)

12. if you have a work history, put your personal profile here

13. other information may include driving licence, languages, community activities, smoker or non-smoker, able to work unsociable hours

14. two references (teacher, tutor, minister, doctor, youth worker, previous employment, a professional person).

Figure 13 shows a model chronological CV.

EFFECTIVE LETTER WRITING

- ensure a good business layout
- keep it brief and to the point

Covering letters

A covering letter is used when sending off your CV or an application form for a specifically advertised vacancy. Pointers to bear in mind:

- put your full address and telephone number in the letter

- ideally address your letter to a named person if stated in the advert, if there is no name put "Dear Sir/Madam"

- If you address the letter to a named person, sign off "Yours sincerely", if you address the letter "Dear Sir/Madam, sign off "Yours faithfully"

- the first paragraph of the letters should state what you are replying to and where and when seen

Name: Robert Smith

Address: 19 Chestnut Avenue
Treetown
Woodshire

Telephone: 0111 64295

Date of Birth: 17.10.1955

Education: Queens Park Secondary School
Brighton
1967-1971

Professional Qualifications:

Heidelburg UK Certificate (K Line)	1981
City & Guilds Advanced Certificate in Letterpress and Photogravure	1976
City & Guilds Basic Craft Certificate in Letterpress	1974

Fig. 13. A chronological CV model
(by kind permission of Robert).

Employment History:

Ponders Print
Brighton
1995 -
Litho machine minder   Heidelburg MO 2 colour

L S Fontwell
Lewes
1987 - 1995
Litho machine minder   Heidelburg KORD
                             Heidelburg GTO single colour
                             Heidelburg MO 2 colour
                             Heidelburg Speedmaster 2 colour
                             Heidelburg Speedmaster 4 colour

Eastern Publishers
Brighton
1971 - 1987
Letterpress machine minder   Thompson Platten
                             Verticle Miehle
                             Heidelburg Double Crown
                             Tirfing
Litho machine minder   Heidelburg KORD

Personal Profile:

I would describe myself as a good team member but also someone who enjoys working under their own autonomy. My experience has taught me to be patient, disciplined and efficient in precise work. I am willing to work irregular hours and am always happy to learn new machines.

References   Alan Smith   John Black
                  Ponder Print   L S Fontwell
                  Brighton   Lewes

- the second paragraph is your sales pitch containing relevant skills, strengths and experience

- the third paragraph is where you indidate your availability for interview and say you have enclosed your CV

- whenever you put something else in an envelope other than the letter always put ENC. at the bottom left hand corner of your letter.

Spec letters

Speculative letters are a form of cold calling. They are written to companies with the intention of finding work — only not directly asking for a job. There are four good reasons for writing speculative letters.

1. When replying to an advertised vacancy, you may be one of fifty applicants, when you write a spec letter, you may be one of two or three people doing the same thing.

2. Your spec letter may arrive when a vacancy needs filling but is not yet advertised (only a very small percentage of vacancies are filled through advertisements).

3. Your spec letter is likely to show initiative and could be placed on file for the next suitable vacancy to arise.

4. You are so good at selling yourself that you create a need for your services.

Some pointers to bear in mind when sending spec letters:

- tailor-make the letters
- the letter is a business proposition
- research the organisation
- identify in the letter where you fit in
- target the letter at a named individual
- get a meeting
- don't ask for a job, ask for information

- the first paragraph of the letters should state who you are, what you do and why you are writing
- the second paragraph is your sales pitch containing relevant skills, strengths and experience
- the third paragraph is where you request a meeting and indicate the enclosed resume.

FILLING IN APPLICATION FORMS

When you apply for a job, either you will be asked to send in a CV or you will be sent an application form. If you have prepared your CV, the details from this can be transferred across to the application form. Figure 16 shows a typical application form.

ATTENDING AN INTERVIEW

The interview is your opportunity to sell yourself directly to a company. When people go for interviews, they tend to give away their power. Granted, the interviewer is the one who can hire and fire you. Equally, you can vote with your feet and turn the job down. You too have power to say no or yes. You have an equal right to ask questions of any prospective employer. Questions you may be asked include:

- Why do you want to work for this company?
- What are your future ambitions?
- Why do you want to work in this type of occupation?
- Why did you leave your last job?
- What would your last employer say about you?
- What do you feel you could contribute to this organisation?
- Where do you see yourself working in three years' time?
- What would you consider as your strengths?
- What would you consider as your weaknesses?
- Are there any questions you would like to ask?

Mr J White
Centre Manager
Anywhere Training Centre
Somewhere Street
Brighton

Tel: 01273 123456

Dear Mr White

As a professional trainer in career development skills, I would like to offer my services to your organisation. I am currently seeking to expand my contractual work and would welcome the opportunity of working with minority groups seeking employment.

I have extensive experience in working with long-term unemployed personnel giving guidance and facilitating training groups. Additional skills include the design of open learning systems for career development and the writing of a book, Surviving Redundancy.

Should there be any relevant opportunities, I would be happy to meet with you at your convenience. I enclose a brief resume of my experience.

I look forward to hearing from you.

Yours sincerely

Laurel Alexander Cert Ed., Assoc IPD

enc.

Fig. 14. A speculative letter.

Mrs Tricket
Personnel
Anywhere Training Centre
Somewhere Street
Brighton
Tel: 01273 123456

Dear Mrs Tricket

Re: Training Administrator

I would like to express my interest with reference to the above position, advertised in the Brighton Echo on Thursday 3 August.

At present I work for Adams Secretarial College as registration administrator and have been in this post for five years. I have just completed my NVQ Business Administration Level 3 and am currently seeking new opportunities and additional responsibility where I can develop my skills and knowledge.

The position of Training Administrator with your company is therefore of great interest to me and I would welcome the opportunity of an interview. As requested, please find enclosed my CV. I look forward to hearing from you.

Yours sincerely

Mary Smith

Enc.

Fig. 15. A letter of application.

MR/MS/MRS/MISS	NATIONALITY
SURNAME	OTHER NAMES
AGE	DATE OF BIRTH
TEL NUMBER	ARE YOU REGISTERED DISABLED?
ADDRESS	

EDUCATION School/College	Dates	Examinations/Results

EMPLOYMENT Employer	Dates	Responsibilities

STATE WHY YOU THINK YOU ARE SUITABLE FOR THIS POST

Fig. 16. A specimen application form.

Selling Yourself

- How would you describe your health?
- How did you achieve your professional qualifications?
- Why were you selected for redundancy?
- What have you been doing in the period you have been unemployed?
- Tell me more about yourself.
- Give me three reasons why I should employ you.
- Give me a brief outline of your career to date.

Psychometric tests

These types of test are designed to gauge:

- personal qualities, *eg* leadership
- interests
- personality, *eg* conscientiousness
- aptitudes, *eg* specific abilities
- general intellectual ability.

The tests are endorsed by the British Psychological Society and administered by a qualified person. The objective of the test is to further affirm your suitability for a post.

Your successful interview checklist

- research the company and know what the position is about
- ask questions
- be enthusiastic without going overboard
- shake hands on entering and leaving
- look the interviewer/panel in the eye with a smile

- sit relaxed in chair — don't slouch — don't sit forward
- think professional
- don't smoke
- don't joke around aside from pleasantries
- take a pen and note pad out at the beginning of the interview and make occasional notes
- leave your coat in the reception area
- keep your jewellery to a minium but wear significant earrings (or tie)
- have clean, well manicured nails (with either clear or no polish)
- have clean hair tied back or put up
- make-up in natural soft colours
- carry an attaché case or leather file
- choose natural rather than loud colours
- look current but not trendy
- avoid flashy scarves or accessories
- wear court shoes as opposed to stilettos, flatties or boots.

Self assessment
What would you do if:

- they had lost your application form/CV?
- you were prepared to shake hands but no one offers?
- you were called by an entirely different name by the interviewer?

No one can sell you better than you can yourself. Your CV, spec letters, applications forms, the telephone call and the interview are tools of your trade as a job-seeker. As well as your tools, having pride in your achievements and experience will help to motivate you in your sales pitch. You do have a work history, you have life experience, you may have a family — you are someone. Remember, if you are not successful this time, it's your skills that are being rejected — **not you personally**. You only need one job. Maybe it's the next one — keep going.

CASE STUDIES

Angela builds up her image
Angela has built up an excellent range of communications skills through her secretarial/administration work. Her image and style are too feminine and she is aware of the need to build up a more professional image for a woman.

Robert is out of practice
As Robert hasn't had an interview for 15 years, he is anxious about what to do and say. In the print trade, most jobs are heard about on the grapevine and initial contact is nearly always by phone and followed by an informal interview.

Alan needs to open up a little
Alan's work depends upon his communication skills. His image is current and he enjoys looking good. He rarely allows his emotions to surface, making him sometimes come across as a terse communicator.

DISCUSSION POINTS

1. Consider the interviews that you have had in the past. What do you think of how you were interviewed? If you had been the interviewer, how would you have conducted the session?

2. How does your image change when you're with different people or when you do different things?

3. Explore your views on the following statement, 'listening is a natural activity'.

9
Training and Education

WHAT IS LEARNING?

Tell me and I forget
Show me and I may remember
Involve me and I'll understand

Learning is for a life. Whether we attend a formal or informal course, we are constant students and teachers. Each one of us develops and grows through our life experiences and we pass this learning onto others through our inter-actions. Work-related study has never been so easy as it is now. There are so many opportunities to learn. I have always enjoyed teaching and training adults because of the exchange of experience and wisdom. As an adult, you have a great deal to offer when you come on a course as a student. In return, you've the opportunity to grow and develop as a person, a chance to learn new skills and gain fresh knowledge. Ultimately it is an opportunity for you to gain confidence in yourself and discover new skills. From here you can set goals for a fresh career start and begin to take greater pride in your achievements.

When we were at school, we had to learn what we were told. We may have had limited choice over subject matter. Consequently, our motivations could have been low. We may not have been good at a subject, we may have disliked a particular teacher, we may have been humiliated or laughed at. Many adults have negative memories of their schooldays and returning to study or education can seem daunting.

However, as adults we have choice and freedom. We can set our own goals and work out strategies for achieving them. We can take control of our learning and this opens up wide and exciting fields of opportunity and discovery.

Did you know:

- training amongst the self employed has risen steadily since 1984

Training and Education

- those between 35-44 receive more training than those aged between 25-34

- employers increasingly rely on 'growing their own' trained workforce.

Education and training means

- updating existing skills and knowledge
- learning new skills
- gaining qualifications
- networking
- showing you are using your time well during unemployment
- being stimulated
- being challenged
- gaining confidence
- building a routine
- meeting new people — a sense of belonging.

Useful learning skills

- problem solving
- taking action
- questioning
- finding information
- selecting
- synthesis
- memorising
- observation.

Getting help and support while learning

- if in doubt — ask
- use your peers
- improve your learning skills
- improve your study skills.

Developing study skills

Planning your time
You may need to draw up a timetable based on allocation of available time for revision and consolidation. Family commitments and social life

need to be taken into account. Try and set aside a period for reading each day, ideally taking notes at the same time.

Using textbooks
You can quickly get the feel of a book by obtaining an overview from the preface, by selecting a topic from the index and noting the author's methods of dealing with it. When looking at a new textbook:

- look at chapter headings
- look at section headings in each chapter
- skim some sentences and look at diagrams.

Other methods of reading include:

- 'active reading' from a textbook using the 3R method — read, recite, record

- Robinson's SQ3r method — survey, question, read, recite, review

- Pauk's OK5R method — overview, key ideas, read, record, recite, review, reflect.

The marking of your own textbooks to assist in memorisation is a good learning aid. Read sections or paragraphs fully before underlining and use symbols in consistent fashion to mark matter requiring further study.

Hints for remembering
Recital, review and practice in retrieval contribute to long-term remembering. Seek associations within the subject area:

Verbal	—	group things together
	—	pair things together
	—	link with things you already know
	—	make up a story linking things together
Visual	—	group things together and visualise them
	—	write a list and visualise it
Repetition	—	write out the words a number of times
	—	repeat aloud a number of times
	—	read over and over again.

Translate what you read into mind movies. Make them as clear and graphic as possible and play them through in your head. Always try to visualise what you want to remember. A useful technique for remembering key facts involves getting yourself into a state of relaxation and then seeing in your imagination the key words you want to remember being written by a giant hand. Each word should be written in capital letters with a contrast between the words and the paper on which they are written. Work on a maximum of five words at a time.

Conditions for good recall

- you tend to remember the last thing you read
- the more you test yourself the more you learn
- the more you concentrate the more you learn
- the more important the material is to you, the more you learn
- your state of mind affects what you learn
- the more you can relate the material to be learned to other things, the more you learn.

Search for pattern and structure and do not learn everything by rote. Understanding is a more valuable aid in long-term remembering. Finally, be keen.

Note taking

Why	— for reference, revision, to restructure meaning, as an *aide memoire*, to outline essay
Where	— in note books, binders, on cards
When	— after reading, while reading, during or after lecture/radio/TV.
How	— type, write, use standard or personal abbreviation, use colour, diagrams, sentences, symbols, headings, underline, numbering
What	— main ideas, key words, essential details, sources, references.

Self assessment

- I enjoy learning   Yes/No

- I like to memorise facts   Yes/No
- I enjoy making notes   Yes/No
- I enjoy finding things out for myself   Yes/No
- I learn better in a group   Yes/No
- I learn better on my own   Yes/No

Ask yourself

- What do I want to learn?
- When do I want to learn?
- Who do I want to learn with?
- Why do I want to learn?
- Where do I want to learn?
- How do I want to learn?

Checklist

Do I want:

1. a course which prepares me for paid work by helping to build my confidence?

2. a course which gives me practice with interviews and jobsearch?

3. a further education or training qualification so that I can apply for jobs which I am not qualified for at present?

4. a course for leisure?

5. a course which will prepare me to set up on my own?

6. a course which will enable me to acquire new skills or retrain so that I can change direction?

7. a course which will help me to update my skills and knowledge so that I can return to my profession?

BASIC EDUCATION

This is useful for improving basic skills such as reading, writing or maths. It is also useful for people whose first language is not English.

ESOL

These initials stand for English for Speakers of Other Languages. The courses are designed to build confidence in handling English in everyday situations.

FURTHER EDUCATION

Further education and tertiary colleges offer work-related courses for both post-school leavers and mature students. Courses run full and part-time. Academic qualifications include GCSEs, A levels and A/S levels. Courses might include beauty therapy, hairdressing, engineering, furniture restoration, training, building or computer technology.

ADULT EDUCATION

Your local further education college is likely to have an adult education department. Often sixth form colleges run adult education classes as well. The traditional view of adult education is one of afternoon classes run for old ladies on flower arranging. In reality, courses run on a weekly basis, usually for two hours a time. Course are held in the morning, afternoon and evening. Often there are Saturday classes as well. Subjects range from leisure interests through to computers and word processing and go on to qualification and certificate levels.

If you are thinking about a career change, it might be an idea to consider a leisure course. The costs and commitment are low — and it might open new doors. If you are on benefit, you are likely to get a substantial reduction in fees. Courses might include massage, aromatherapy, computers, counselling, catering, art or languages.

The Workers' Educational Association
The WEA runs part-time courses in response to local needs.

ACCESS COURSES

These courses provide access to higher education for students who do not have the formal qualifications for entry. They are foundation courses and are run on a flexible basis with additional help in study skills. Some courses are linked to a particular degree course and will give you a greater opportunity of being offered a place at university upon completion.

HIGHER EDUCATION

Universities offer courses leading to degrees or Higher National Certificates or Diplomas. Mature students are specifically encouraged. Courses might include accounting, chemistry, computing, electronics and management.

OPEN AND DISTANCE LEARNING

The Open University
The OU offers certificate, diploma and degree courses to anyone. You do not need qualifications to be accepted onto a course and learning takes place via the TV, radio, textbooks and other material. Each student has a local OU tutor and there is usually a summer school to back up the learning process.

National Extension College
This registered charity offers courses on study skills, GCSEs, A levels and degrees in conjunction with the University of London. There are no entry qualifications.

GOVERNMENT SCHEMES

TECs
These initials stand for Training and Enterprise Councils. They are responsible for government training programmes for people who wish to return to work or who are unemployed.

Government Scheme — Training for Work
If you have been out of work for six months or more, this programme provides the opportunity of gaining an NVQ and work experience.

Government Scheme — Learning for Work
This scheme is for long-term unemployed people and offers the opportunity to follow work-related, full-time courses without loss of benefit.

HOW TO FIND OUT ABOUT COURSES

TAPs
These initials stand for Training Access Points, which provide computer guidance information on local training and educational opportunities.

Careers Office
This service is available in most towns and provides advice and information for young people and adults.

Jobcentres
The local Jobcentre will be able to provide information on government training and re-training schemes in your area.

Citizens Advice Bureau
Your local CAB should be able to provide guidance in the types of courses available in your area and possible contact points plus advice on dealing with debts.

Educational Institutions
Adult education centres, further education colleges, polytechnics and universities all publish a prospectus at least once a year if not more. Some institutions have open days prior to enrolment where you can talk to the tutors.

Library
Most libraries have reference sections which may have substantial course information. Leaflets and prospectuses may also be found there.

QUALIFICATIONS

Awarding bodies

BTEC (The Business & Technology Education Council)
These courses are a mixture of educational and work-based experiences delivered in a variety of ways, *eg* full-time, open learning, block or day release and evening class.

C & G (City & Guilds)
These courses are available in full or part-time and evening class modes. They come in three different levels to reflect levels of proficiency.

RSA (Royal Society for the Encouragement of Arts Manufactures and Commerce)
Students do not need prior qualifications to take these courses.

NVQs

National Vocational Qualifications are the qualifications of the future. They are recognised both in this country and in Europe and can be transferred across the vocational sphere. NVQs are employer led, which means that the lead bodies (the official body which heads each vocational sphere) work with industry and commerce to set the national standards for competence. NVQs are made up of units which can be built up over a period of time. You can choose which unit you wish to do and gain a certificate for each unit. Assessment is usually work-based and you can take an NVQ at your own speed.

Learning jargon

APL

These initials stand for Accredited Prior Learning. This means that your existing skills and knowledge can now be recognised and used to help you gain a qualification.

CATS

These initials stand for Credit Accumulation & Transfer Scheme. This means you can get credit for learning that happened in different places. These credits can then build towards a qualification.

Projects

- find out what courses are available that are of interest to you and whether you have the qualifications to do them

- find out if the qualifications on offer lead to a job

- find out the job market following qualification.

COSTS AND FUNDING

If you are considering returning to education, you may need to take the following costs into account:

- course fee
- exam fee
- books and equipment
- travel
- childcare.

Grants

The amount of money awarded for living expenses is income linked. For students living at home, this will be related to the income of parents. For those who have been married at least two years before course commencement, this will be related to their partner's income.

- mandatory grants are available for full-time courses in higher education

- discretionary grants are available for full-time further education courses

- if you are over 26 and have earned at least £12,000 in the three years prior to a course, you may qualify for a Mature Student grant.

Postgraduate Awards

These come in the form of a bursary or a studentship. To qualify, you need a first degree.

Claiming benefit

- if you have not been in full-time education for three months and are living on Income Support, you can study for up to 21 hours without your benefit being affected

- if you receive Income Support or Unemployment Benefit you will **not** be able to attend a full-time further or higher education course and continue to receive benefit.

Career development loans

This type of loan has evolved through the Department of Employment and certain major banks. You can borrow £200 - £8,000 to cover a percentage of course fees and the cost of books and childcare. You can take a full-time, part-time, open or distance learning course as long as it is related to the kind of work you want to do and lasts no longer than two years.

STAR

If you have been unemployed for more than six months and you have an interview arranged, the STAR scheme will offer a prospective employer £700 towards your initial training. Contact the Jobcentre to find out more.

Sources of financial assistance

Tax relief	— if taking a NVQ — covers tuition and most materials
Career development loans	— covers 80% of course fees plus materials
Council tax concessions	— students are exempt
Discretionary awards	— FE grants
Educational trusts and charities	— usually small part-funding
HE access funds	
FE access funds	
Trade union sponsorship	— small grants
European Social Fund	— reduced course fees, allowances for childcare and materials.

Course checklist

- What entry qualifications do I need?
- How long does the course last?
- How many hours of study are involved both at college and at home?
- What is the cost?
- Are grants available?
- What are the financial effects on benefits?
- What can I do about childcare provision?
- How far will I have to travel?
- How do I apply?

CASE STUDIES

Angela updates her business skills
Angela is considering going into business with a partner, as a financial adviser. Most of the qualifications required by law are being obtained by her partner. However, she needs to update her business skills and enrols on several further education courses, using her redundancy money to fund them.

Robert gets to grips with computers
Robert's blind spot is with computers. Printing presses are being updated with CPCs (computer based technology) and he wants to become more familiar with computers to conquer his fear. He takes a Saturday workshop as an introduction to computers at his local adult education college.

Alan strengthens his portfolio

Alan wants to go self employed as a portfolio person. He is considering a copyrighting and desk-top publishing business, teaching marketing, sales and advertising and writing about it. He opts for a correspondence course in writing and taking a certificate in education with his local college.

DISCUSSION POINTS

1. What advantages are there to learning later in life?

2. Explore your personal motivations for learning.

3. How might the effects of redundancy and/or long-term unemployment affect someone's learning curve?

10
Your Way Forward

USING WHAT YOU HAVE

During your working life you have had many experiences, built up many skills and acquired much knowledge. Then you were made redundant — but this event doesn't take away who you are or what you have done. You are still the same person — a little battered perhaps, but still the same.

Where you are now
This book has been designed to add to your building blocks of self knowledge. We have explored:

The first few weeks
Reacting to the redundancy — saying goodbye — dealing with loss — coping with the first few days

Organising your finances
Getting something for nothing — defining your needs and wants

Coping with change
Stress management — positive thinking — time management — physical fitness — healthy eating

Redefining your value system
Why do you work — work values and motivations — skills assessment

Your career development strategy
Researching the job market — returning to study — organising your jobsearch strategy — making speculative contacts — using the media — networking — creating your own job

Overcoming constraints
Sexism — ageism — literacy and numeracy — dependants — location and travel — a criminal record — lack of experience — the benefit loop — the economic climate — health — ethnic origin — job competition — need for higher income — beliefs and values — lack of confidence

Choosing a mode of work
Term-time working — working from home — the portfolio person — temporary work — flexitime — jobshare — contract work — part time work — self employment

Selling yourself
Verbal and non verbal communication — image and style — reading the job advertisement — using the telephone — the CV — writing letters — application forms — interviews

Training and education
Study skills — basic education — further education — adult education — access courses — higher education — open learning — government schemes — qualifications — funding

What now?
The rest of this chapter explores:

- empowerment
- using effective thinking
- giving yourself positive strokes
- improving your self image
- your philosophy toward life
- goal setting
- action planning
- endings and beginnings.

You have now begun to more deeply assess who you are, what you have and what you know so that you are in a more powerful position to move forward into new employment that more accurately represents the real you.

LETTING GO OF BEING A VICTIM

No one is out to get you. The world is not deliberately doing you down.

The government hasn't got your name on their hit list. God isn't out to make your life a misery. You are a powerful individual going through a time of change because of redundancy. You don't have to like it, of course, but you now have a major opportunity to grow and develop.

There is a school of philosophy which believes:

I'm OK, you're OK

I'm OK, you're not OK   *I'm not OK, you're not OK*

- *I'm not OK, you're not OK* means I feel victimised, miserable and hopeless and so do you; there's no hope for any of us, so why bother. Neither of us wins.

- *I'm OK, you're not OK* means I'll take from you so that I feel better because you feel more awful than me. I win and you lose.

- *I'm OK, you're OK* means I feel empowered and respect myself and others and I know that you feel the same way. We are in control of our lives. We both win.

It is up to you to take advantage of every opportunity that comes your way. If there aren't enough — **create them**.

TAKING RESPONSIBILITY

You are the only person who can make a difference in your life. Other people can contribute to your success and sense of well-being, but at the end of the day, it is attitude not aptitude that makes altitude. It is your state of mind and creative approach to employment that will bring a positive response. No one owes you a living and no other person can give you something that you aren't prepared to give yourself. Maintaining this attitude takes determination and discipline and there is no doubt that there will be times when you feel resentful, frustrated and angry. That's OK. You can cope with these negative feelings — you have a right to feel and express them appropriately. You'll feel better if you do express them. However, they won't last and you will feel hopeful again. All you need is one person to say 'I have pleasure in being able to offer you the position of'.

When you take responsibility for your life and what happens to you, you are no longer a victim. Sometimes when you wait for that phone call or letter asking you for an interview or telling you that you've got the job, you may feel as if all the power in the world belongs to the employers — **but it doesn't**. You have the power. You have the power to feel up or down, positive or negative, fearful or excited. You can feel **empowered**. You are in control. You cannot control other people or their responses, but you can control your own behaviour, thoughts and feelings. If you don't like waiting for others, keep pro-active in your job-search. If you don't like being rejected, keep reminding yourself of your skills and strengths; if you don't like not having a job, find other meaningful pursuits while you wait.

Creating your ideal job treasure map
Your treasure map should show you in your ideal scene with your goal fully realised. Place a photograph of yourself in the centre of a large sheet and show yourself doing your ideal job, in your ideal location. Cut out pictures and words from magazines. Show the situation as if it already exists. Be positive and use colour to create impact. Put an affirmation on the treasure map. 'Here I am working as a graphic designer in a light, airy office with people I like, earning good money and feeling good about myself'.

USING EFFECTIVE THINKING SKILLS

Effective thinking means taking responsibility for your own choices, accurate perception of self and others and using visual thinking skills. There are certain conditions which contribute to negative thinking:

Overestimating
This is when we overestimate the odds of a negative outcome to a situation: 'I'll never get an interview when they hear I was made redundant'.

Overgeneralising
This is when we falsely assume that one bad experience will become the norm: 'No one ever responds to my CV'.

Filtering
This is focusing on one negative aspect of a situation so that we ignore any positive aspects.

Emotional reasoning
This is a tendency to evaluate something illogically, totally on the basis of feelings: 'He didn't like me — I could tell. He kept staring — I feel awful.'

'Should' statements
These are the trademark of your inner-perfectionist. By imposing the word 'should' on yourself, you are lowering your self esteem. Following the inner-perfectionist telling you what you should do, your inner-critic then comes in to tell you how badly you are doing it.

Using constructive inner speech
Inner speech occurs as we become conscious of our thoughts. We can use affirmations to affirm the positive rather than the negative:

Before an interview	— 'My body is relaxed and I feel confident.'
During the interview	— 'I am calm and in control.'
	— Speak slowly and clearly. I am good enough.'
After the interview	— 'I am doing very well. I am learning a lot. I am ready for the next time.'
While waiting for a job offer	— 'I am a worthwhile person. The right job is coming my way.'

Making choices
A further development of using powerful inner speech is using your power of choice to tune out of the negative and into the positive:

Negative inner speech	*Positive inner speech*
I am afraid of being unemployed	I am excited about getting a new job
I don't have any money	I have enough to pay the essentials
I am off course	I am on the path
I can't get a job	I will get a job
I am too old	I enjoy getting older
I don't count	I count

I am filled with self doubt	I am confident
I can't do anything	I am always learning new skills
I feel useless	I do something useful every day

Preventing and managing problems

An effective jobsearch strategy involves being able to solve problems. Knowing the right person to contact, anticipating hurdles, overcoming barriers and researching all take problem solving skills.

Analyse your problem
- be specific
- who
- what
- when
- where
- why.

Brainstorming
- don't judge your thoughts
- freewheel
- let as many ideas as possible come.

Improve or discard
- be ruthless
- be critical.

GIVING YOURSELF POSITIVE STROKES

When we have been made redundant, our sense of self esteem wobbles and it is then that we need someone to tell us how brilliant we are, how loveable and how much we are needed. Sadly, there isn't always someone around who can do this, so we have to learn to do it for ourselves. We need to learn to be our own best friend. When others praise us, this is the icing on the cake, but ultimately, we need to be able to do it for ourselves.

Project

On a large sheet of paper, write out all the things you like about yourself. Put it up in a place where you can see it every day and keep adding any new strengths that you discover.

TEN STEPS TO FEELING POSITIVE

1. Get rid of the word 'should' from your vocabulary — use 'could'.

2. Short circuit negative mind-messages as soon as they start by using the word 'stop'.

3. Think about what is going well in your life.

4. Practise going from anxiety to an active and problem solving framework.

5. Create opportunities.

6. Learn to recognise what is redundant about your own attitudes.

7. Investigate new interests — try things you've never done before.

8. Before you fall asleep at night find at least one thing in each day that was enjoyable.

9. Stop criticising yourself and learn to like who you are.

10. Laugh at yourself a little more.

Remember

- It's up to you to take your life and use it.
- Nobody owes you anything.
- You can decide to make something of what you have and improve upon it, or you can choose to let things get you down.
- As one door closes, another opens — providing you look for it.

IMPROVING YOUR SELF IMAGE

Your self image is the way you see yourself and how you feel about yourself. Affirmations and creative visualisation are excellent ways of creating a more positive self image. Think of specific qualities you appreciate about yourself. In the same way that you might boost up a friend when they are down while still seeing their faults, you can appreciate yourself for all that you are while still being aware that there are ways you need to develop. Begin to tell yourself:

- I am talented, intelligent and creative
- I am willing to be happy and successful
- I express myself freely, fully and easily
- I don't have to try to please anyone else; I like myself and that's what counts.

It is often more effective to do this type of affirmation in the second person, using your own name:
'Sheila, you are a brilliant and interesting person. I like you very much.'

The anchor trick
Sit down in a quiet place, close your eyes and relax. Bring to mind a time when you felt successful and confident. Recall the scene in as much detail as possible. Where, when, how? Who else was there? What was said? When you have got the positive, strong feelings in your mind, anchor them by clasping your left shoulder or upper arm with your right hand. When you need to feel confident and positive, in an interview for example, clasping your shoulder or upper arm should re-affirm those good feelings instantly.

DEVELOPING A PHILOSOPHICAL ATTITUDE

Developing a philosophical attitude is like preparing a flower bed for new growth. Our beliefs form the substance of positive and healthy development. Our philosophy toward life sustains us through difficulty. It is helpful to develop a positive but realistic philosophy towards work, employment and material resources.

Project
Consider the following:

- We create our own reality by what we perceive to be true

- We always have a choice
- Change the inner and the outer will follow.
- Positive energy attracts positive experiences.

YOUR POSITIVE ACHIEVEMENTS JOURNAL

You may find it useful to keep a Positive Achievement Journal throughout your jobsearch. This journal will become a real sign that you are achieving tasks and developing your jobsearch skills. In the journal, record all your negative feelings and then try to offset them with positive achievements. Rule a page into two halves. On the left hand side, record:

- the date
- the situation
- the nature of your negative behaviour
- the result of your behaviour.

On the right hand side record:

- the date
- the situation
- the nature of your positive behaviour
- the result of your behaviour.

Aim to reduce the number of left hand entries and increase the number of right hand entries. Try to record one positive achievement each day.

SETTING AND ACHIEVING GOALS

Goal setting is the way we measure achievement. When we achieve in part or whole, we feel good about ourselves:

- be specific
- set short, medium and long-term goals
- set different types of goals — financial, educational and creative
- be realistic
- uncover and remove internal barriers
- build a support network
- review goals

- evaluate goals
- revise goals.

Use Figures 17 and 18 as a guide towards setting goals and drafting an action plan for yourself.

ENDINGS AND BEGINNINGS

I have enjoyed writing this book. It has motivated me and I hope it motivates you. My working life has been full of endings and beginnings. I have had many jobs, worked in different environments, been both employed by others and self employed. I took my first qualification course when I was 29. I have sent out so many spec letters and CVs, I could paper my hallway. But I have always enjoyed my working life (most of it anyway).

I am constantly challenged by change. I am always growing, developing and learning. I will never have a job for life because there are no jobs for life — but I will always be in work because there will always be work if you look hard enough. When times are hard and work is a bit thin on the ground and not much money is coming in, I'm thinking of the next plan, the next idea, the next spec letter, the next bit of learning, the next pay cheque. When I lose heart, I talk to someone, I cry, I thump a cushion, I moan and moan — then I try again. And I work again.

So will you, I promise. Persevere and believe in yourself. I believe in you and I have never met you. Good luck!

CASE STUDIES

Angela drives towards success
Angela has a strong, almost fatalistic, philosophical attitude toward life. Her belief system is positive and she is a woman who believes in action. She has now been in partnership as a self employed financial consultant for five years and they are considering opening another branch of their management services.

Robert gains confidence in himself
Robert has to work towards building a philosophical foundation. He tends to perceive himself through the eyes of others. He is a conscientious and hard worker, but he tends to focus on the negative in a situation. He is learning to value himself more through accepting his skills

and knowledge as a printer. Following his redundancy, he was headhunted by another company and stayed with them for eight years. Recently, he made a conscious choice to change jobs voluntarily which reflected the development of his maturity and control of choice. Consequently, following his networking activities, he has been offered another job as a printer and made an excellent career move.

Alan re-evaluates his life

Following a succession of redundancies, Alan has re-evaluated his life completely. He acknowledges his lifestyle was too stressful and competitive. He is now a freelance marketing consultant which he does part-time, he lectures for local colleges and is now writing a book on self-employment for the over 50s. He allows more time for leisure and is building more meaningful relationships into his life.

DISCUSSION POINTS

1. Evaluate how you make decisions in your life. How can you improve the quality of your decision-making?

2. Identify your thinking skill weaknesses.

3. How can you increase your skills of self-perception?

MY GOALS

Job work	☐	full-time or part-time for a salary
Supplementary work	☐	a guaranteed income done in addition to essential unpaid work or as a supplement to a partner's income
Maintenance work	☐	unpaid work done for family and the broader community
Self-employment	☐	
Working abroad	☐	
Time out	☐	
Further education	☐	part-time study .... full-time study ....
Access course	☐	part-time study .... full-time study ....
Higher education	☐	part-time study .... full-time study ....
Adult education	☐	
Open learning	☐	
Private training	☐	part-time study .... full-time study ....

Fig. 17. Your goals record.

Information required:

- AE ☐
- FE ☐
- ACCESS ☐
- HE ☐
- Open learning ☐
- Benefits ☐
- Childcare ☐
- Government schemes ☐
- Private training ☐
- Self employment ☐

Skills development

- Application forms ☐
- Letter writing ☐
- CVs ☐
- Interview techniques ☐
- Image and presentation ☐
- Jobsearch ☐
- Study skills ☐
- Confidence building ☐

OBJECTIVE

Develop an action plan for your career development you could begin achieving within three months from now.

Actions Each clearly identifiable and measurable	Organisations to contact	Target date	Date when step taken
1.			
2.			
3.			
4.			
5.			
6.			
7.			
8.			
9.			
10.			

Fig. 18. Your action plan.

Glossary

Action plan. This occurs as part of the process of change. When we have thought through a course of action, we need to plan the specific steps needed to make that action happen.

Ageism. An attitude adopted by those who believe that age affects a person's ability to do a job well. Employees can be prejudiced against specific age groups when filling a vacancy.

Aide memoire. A book or document which serves as an aid to the memory.

Aptitude. A natural talent for a skill.

Assignment. A task allocated to a student reflecting their learning.

Behavioural. This term refers to how we behave, our actions, what we do.

Benefit system. The formal system put in place by the government which allocates financial resources for special needs, *eg* if a person is unemployed, disabled, has a family etc.

Block/day release. When you are in full-time employment and studying for a qualification, it is usually required that you are released from your work one day or more per week to attend college.

Brainstorm. This creative process occurs when you need to think of ideas. A time limit is usually placed on the process and the objective is to let as many thoughts out as possible in the time, without judgement.

Business plan. A lengthy document required by someone from whom you want to borrow money if you wish to work for yourself.

Business rate. This is an annual sum of money paid to the local council for rates due on your business premises.

Career counselling. This is a one-to-one process with a trained counsellor who is able to give guidance and possibly assess your career development.

Career development. This is a personal path that we follow which involves the carefully laid out development of skills and knowledge.

Cash flow. This refers to the monies available for expenditure when in business for yourself.

Glossary

Catchment area. When you are searching for work, there may be a specific geographical area that you want to work within.

Cliché. A stereotyped comment or hackneyed phrase.

Claimant advisers. These are personnel who work in Jobcentres. They are available to help with any benefit queries and vacancy advice.

Company name registry. If you want to start a limited company, you will have to place the name with this register.

Concurrent life crisis. Periodically, we face life crises — death, illness, redundancy or divorce. A concurrent life crisis is when there is more than one trauma occurring at the same time.

Conditioning. This term refers to our habitual, learnt responses which form the basis for our thoughts, feelings and behaviours today.

Consolidation. As we go through various learning processes, we accumulate skills and knowledge. There comes a time when we have reached our limit of absorbing new facts and we need to consolidate what we have learnt.

Constructive criticism. This is a form of feedback which offers helpful advice. It is empowering and positive. Destructive criticism involves putting people down via a negative attitude.

Consumer. A purchaser of goods or services.

Copyright. The exclusive right given by law for a term of years to a writer or designer etc to makes copies of his or her original work.

Credit control. Information and control of customers' credit limits when in business for yourself.

Dependants. This term refers to children or aged parents or relatives who are dependent upon us to care for them. This caring role may influence the time we have available for work or study.

Direct mail. This term is used for specifically targeted mail. A mailing list is purchased by a company who then targets various addresses with their sales letter or brochure. A mailing list is comprised of people who share a common interest or goal, *eg* people interested in purchasing shares.

Diversification. Being involved in several projects.

Draft. This refers to a preliminary copy of a document.

Empower. This term refers to a psychological state involving thoughts and emotions. It represents an assertive stance where the individual has a personal sense of power and believes in their right to express themselves appropriately without taking away someone else's power.

Essay. A literary composition on any subject.

Evaluate. To assess.

Expenditure. The spending of money.

Expertise. Expert opinion, skill or knowledge.

Extrapolating. Estimating from known information.

Feedback. The return response to your words or behaviour.

Forum. A meeting for public discussion.

Foundation course. This term usually refers to a university type course and describes a course taken before it begins.

Freewheel. To brainstorm, to think and feel without judgement or boundaries.

Funding. If a student cannot find the cost of a course themselves, full or part-funding may be available from various sources.

Goal setting. Before we take action, we need to plan our goals.

Government schemes. The government has initiated several schemes designed to help with funding courses and finding employment. Your local Jobcentre or TEC will have details.

Hidden agenda. When we communicate with others, we may not always be aware of our motivations. Sometimes we may be aware of what we want out of a situation, but we hide it from others. This is called a hidden agenda.

High interest account. A savings account which offers high interest, from which you usually can't withdraw money quickly.

Inner speech. We are constantly thinking thoughts. Whether we are aware of them or not is another matter. This is inner speech.

Insolvency. A state where the debtor is unable to pay his debts.

Invoice factoring. If you are in business for yourself and are having trouble collecting debts, a factor company buys your debts in return for an immediate cash payment.

Jobcentre. Run by the Civil Service, Jobcentres exist to answer queries on benefit, display local vacancies and advise on training courses.

Journal. A journal is a kind of diary. Not where we record daily events, but where we write or draw out thoughts and feelings about ourselves, others and our place in the world.

Knowledge. Knowledge provides the inner foundation of understanding so that we can develop our skills in action.

Letterbox drops. You may want 5,000 houses in your locality to be aware of your new fish and chip shop. A letterbox drop can be done via your local print shop who will deliver your leaflet alongside two or three others or your local newspaper may take inserts (leaflets).

Mature student. This usually refers to a person returning to study in adulthood.

Media. Publicity sources such as newspapers, TV and radio.

Metamorphosis. A change of character, form or state of being.

Monotonic. When we speak, our voice tone usually goes up and down, slow and fast, quiet and loud. A monotonic voice sounds exactly the same all the time.

Motivation. This refers to our inner drive, our reason for doing something. The reason why we think, feel and behave as we do.

Non-verbal communication. This kind of inter-action is through our body only. Using our hands, body and face, we communicate, often unconsciously, our thoughts and feelings without saying anything.

NVQ. (National Vocational Qualification) is made up of several units. You can gain a certificate for each unit you successfully complete, proving your skill or competence at work.

Objective. A state of mind which reflects a detachment from emotion. An ability to deal with facts uninhibited by feelings.

Patent. A government grant of exclusive rights for the making or selling of new inventions.

Peer. Someone equal in standing or rank or equal in any other respect.

Personal profile. A short statement at the beginning or end of your CV, usually three or four sentences detailing your strengths and skills.

Physiological. Relating to the body.

Preface. The introduction to a book.

Press release. An A4 sheet sent to the editorial department of publications detailing what, why, when, where and who.

Prioritising. Putting things in order of importance.

Pro-active. This term refers to someone who takes action deliberately.

Proficiency. Expertise.

Project management. A managerial term used for the development of specific projects.

Prospectus. The yearly or half-yearly documents detailing courses from adult education, further education and universities.

Public relations (PR). The sophisticated use of communication skills to keep a business in the public eye.

Research. The search to discover using critical investigation.

Resource. Stock that can be drawn upon as a means of support.

Resume. A brief (usually one page), overview of skills, strengths and experience.

Sales pitch. The sales angle taken when selling, *eg* trendy, upmarket, cheap.

Self actualisation. A psychological term referring to reaching our peak of mind, body and spirit.

Self perception. How we perceive ourselves is vital to how we project ourselves to others. If we see ourselves as lacking confidence, then it is likely that we will project ourselves badly and others will react to this. The more positive our self perception, the better image we give to others.

Seminars. A small conference of specialists involving themselves in discussion and intense study.

Sexism. This term applies to those who believe that only men or women can do specific jobs; it also applies to sexual gender and sexual harassment.

Skills assessment. We need to be aware of our skills so that we can sell ourselves through our CV and during an interview. A skills assessment is also necessary when considering a change of career. Skills usually means work-related plus those skills we have built up outside of work that may be relevant, *eg* rock climbing, writing.

Skills. Our ability to perform specific tasks. When we use our skills, we are demonstrating through doing something.

Sole trader. A sole trader is someone who is self employed and working alone.

Stats. Short for statistics.

STD code. The code which comes before your telephone number and designates the area.

Stock control. The maintenance of stock levels and re-ordering.

Study skills. When we are teaching ourselves or being taught, part of the process is using effective study skills which develop the ability for note taking and writing of essays and projects.

Sub-conscious. Part of the mind that is not fully conscious but is able to influence actions.

Summer school. The Open University in particular has summer schools as part of its curriculum. A summer school is usually a residential week of learning held in the middle of the year.

Synopsis. This term refers to an overview of a subject.

Synthesis. A building up of separate elements of a project into a connected whole.

Technology. Computers, information technology, electronics, science.

Tertiary. The next educational institution after secondary school.

Thesis. A document prepared by a student for their degree.

Time out. This refers to a period of time when you are not working, when you are refocusing yourself.

Trade journals. Periodicals relevant to specific trades and professions. Available through professional organisations, the library or a newsagent.

Trade mark registry. Part of the Patent Office. You can register a trade or services mark with them.

Glossary

Training. This type of learning is usually skills based and work-related.

Transition. This is a term used to describe the period of change between two points. When you are made redundant and looking for work, you are in a transitionary period.

Tutorials. When you attend an educational institution, you are likely to be offered tutorials. These are individual or group sessions to discuss your thoughts and feelings about the course and your performance.

Under-pricing. If you are selling goods or a service, there is a danger of under-pricing. If you do this, your profits are unlikely to cover your costs. Also you may give a negative image of your business to potential buyers.

Venture capital. This usually comes via a venture capital sponsor who has money to invest in a business. They also give advice on marketing and organisational structure.

Verbal communication. Speaking and listening to other people.

Victim. Someone who has suffered a bad experience, and who typically feels powerless. Being a victim can be an attitude of mind, and many 'victims' tend to blame other people for their situation and feel uncomfortable when taking personal responsibility.

Work experience. This type of work refers to short-term jobs which form part of a qualification at school or college.

Work history. This term applies to who we have worked for, what we did and when. It is required on your CV and on application forms.

Work motivations. There are always reasons behind why we work — money, power and status being the most common. It is easier to find the right kind of work when we know what our motivations are.

Work-related. Courses being offered are increasingly being related to a working environment.

Useful Addresses

MENTAL AND PHYSICAL HEALTH

National Association of Carers, 58 New Road, Chatham, Kent ME4 4QR.
Opportunities for the Disabled, 1 Bank Building, Prince's Street, London EC2R 8EU. Tel: (0171) 726 4963. Counselling, jobsearch and guidance on training opportunities.

BENEFITS

Social Security freephone line 0800 666555.

CAREER DEVELOPMENT

British Institute of Management, Small Firms Information Centre, Management House, Cottingham Road, Corby, Northamptonshire NN17 1TT, Tel: (01536) 204222.
Business and Professional Women UK, 23 Ansdell Street, Kensington, London W8 5BN. Tel: (0171) 938 1729.
Careers & Occupational Information Centre (COIC), PO Box 348, Bristol BS99 7FE.
Careers for Women, 2 Valentine Place, London SE1 8QH.
Careers Office. See your local *Yellow Pages*.
Equal Opportunities Commission, Overseas House, Quay Street, Manchester M3 3HN. Tel: (0161) 833 9244.
European Commission, Recruitment, Appointments & Promotion Division, DGIX, Commission of the European Communities, 200 Rue de la Loi, B-1049, Brussels, Belgium.
Executive Service, Heatherside House, Park Street, Camberley, Surrey GU15 3NY. A jobsearch agency if you earn more than £15,000 per annum.
Jobsharers, 11a Croft Close, Elford, Staffordshire B79 9BU. Tel: (01827) 383502. A national jobshare register.

National Advisory Centre on Careers for Women, 8th Floor, Artillery House, Artillery Row, London SW1P 1RT.

New Ways to Work, 309 Upper Street, London N1 0PD. Tel: (0171) 226 4026.

Professional and Executive Recruitment (PER). Your local jobcentre.

Skill: National Bureau for Students with Disabilities, 336 Brixton Road, London SW9 7AA. Tel: (0171) 274 0565. Develops opportunities in further and higher education and employment for those with disabilities or learning difficulties.

SELF EMPLOYMENT

British Franchise Association, Thames View, New Town Road, Henley-on-Thames, Oxon RG9 1HG. Tel: (01491) 578049.

Company Registration Office. Companies House, 55 City Road, London EC1Y 1BB. Tel: (0171) 253 9393.

DSS Office. See your local *Yellow Pages*.

Inland Revenue. See your local *Yellow Pages*.

National Federation of Self-Employed and Small Businesses Ltd, 32 St Anne's Road West, Lytham St Anne's, Lancs FY8 1NY. Tel: (01253) 720911.

Rural Development Commission, 141 Castle Street, Salisbury, Wilts SP1 3TP. Tel: (01622) 765222. Grants.

The Trade Marks Registry. Tel: (0171) 438 4700.

Venture Capital Association, 3 Catherine Place, London SW1E 6DX. Tel: (0171) 233 5212.

TRAINING AND EDUCATION

Career Development Loans, Freepost, PO Box 99, Sudbury, Suffolk CO10 6BR. Freephone 0800 585505.

Department of Health, Student Grants Unit, Morcross, Blackpool FY5 3TA. Tel: (01253) 856123. Grants for occupational therapy, physiotherapy, radiography, dentistry.

ECCTIS 2000, Fulton House, Jessop Avenue, Cheltenham, Gloucester GL50 3SH. Tel: (01242) 518724. Computer databases found in colleges, careers offices, adult guidance services and libraries giving information on around 100,000 courses in the UK.

Educational Grants Advisory Service, Family Welfare Association, 501-505 Kingsland Road, London E8.

Educational Liaison Officer, Channel 4 Television, 60 Charlotte Street, London W1P 2AX. Learning from home via the TV.

Insight Information, BBC, Broadcasting House, London W1A 1AA. Learning from home via the TV.

International Training and Recruitment Link, 56 High Street, Harston, Cambridge CB2 5PZ. Tel: (01223) 872747.

Jobcentres. Your local *Yellow Pages*.

Local Education Authorities (LEA). Your local *Yellow Pages*. Mandatory and discretionary grants.

National Association for the Care and Resettlement of Offenders (NACRO) National Education Advisory Service, 567 Barlow Moor Road, Manchester M21 2AE. Information and advice on colleges, courses and grants.

National Council for Vocational Qualifications, 22 Euston Road, London NW1 2BZ. Tel: (0171) 728 1893.

National Extension College, 18 Brooklands Avenue, Cambridge CB2 2HN. Tel: (01223) 316644. Study skills, GCSEs, A levels, degrees, professional studies and languages.

The Open College, St Paul's, 781 Wilmslow Road, Didsbury, Manchester M20 8RW. Tel: (0161) 434 0007. Work related courses including work skills, management and supervision, accountancy, health and care, technology and education and training.

Open College of the Arts, Houndhill, Worsbrough, Barnsley, South Yorkshire S70 6TU. Tel: (01891) 168902. Art and design, creative writing, drawing, garden design, music, painting, photography, sculpture and textiles.

The Open University, PO Box 71, Milton Keynes MK7 6AG.

Project 2000. Your local health authority. Bursaries for nursing.

Radio Publicity, BBC Broadcasting House, London W1A 1AA. Tel: (0171) 580 4468. Learning from home via the radio.

TECs. Training & Enterprise Councils. See your local *Yellow Pages*.

Training Access Points (TAPS), St Mary's House, c/o Moorfoot, Sheffield S1 4PQ.

ETHNIC GROUPS

Fullemploy Training Ltd, 102 Park Village East, London NW1 3SP. Tel: (0171) 387 1222. Vocational training to adults of minority ethnic origin.

PRESENTATION

Colour Me Beautiful, Freepost, London SW8 3NS. Tel: (0171) 627 5211.

Further Reading

HEALTH

Instant Stress Cure, Lyn Marshall (Century Hutchinson, 1988).
Visualization for Change, Patrick Fanning (New Harbinger Publications, 1988).

CAREER DEVELOPMENT

Build Your Own Rainbow, Barrie Hopson and Mike Scally (Mercury, 1991).
Careers and Occupational Information Centre (COIC), PO Box 348, Bristol BS99 7FE. Books and leaflets.
Changing Course, Maggie Smith (Mercury, 1989).
Changing Your Job after 35, Godfrey Golzen (Kogan Page, 1993).
Guidelines for the Redundant Manager (British Institute of Management).
How to Apply for a Job, Judith Johnstone (How To Books 1994).
How to Get that Job, Joan Fletcher (How To Books 1993)
How to Manage Your Career, Roger Jones (How To Books 1994)
How to Start a New Career, Judith Johnstone (How To Books 1994)
How to Work in an Office, Sheila Payne (How To Books 1993)
Job Ideas (COIC).
Job Search Guide (CEPEC Ltd, Princes House, 36 Jermyn Street, London SW1Y 6DN). For executives and professionals.
Jobs for the Over 50s, Linda Greenbury (Piatkus 1994).
Just the Job, John Best (Nicholas Brealey, 1994).
Offbeat Careers, Vivien Donald (Kogan Page 1995).
Test Your Own Aptitude, Jim Barrett and Geoff Williams (Kogan Page 1990).
Women Mean Business, Caroline Bamford & Catherine McCarthy (BBC, 1991).

Working in — (COIC, PO Box 348, Bristol BS99 7FE).
Your Services Are No Longer Required, Christopher Kirkwood (Penguin, 1993).

NEW WAYS OF WORKING

Directory of Jobs & Careers Abroad, Alex Lipinski (Vacation Work).
Guide to Working Abroad, Godfrey Golzen *(Daily Telegraph*/Kogan Page 1994).
How to Start a Business from Home, Graham Jones (How To Books 1994)
How to Start Your Own Business, Jim Green (How To Books 1995).
How to Work from Home, Ian Phillipson (How To Books, 1995).
Job Sharing: A Practical Guide, Pam Walton (Kogan Page, 1990).
National Council for One Parent Families, 255 Kentish Town Road, London NW5 2LX. Tel: (0171) 267 1361. A guide is available helping in various ways.
Working for Yourself, Godfrey Golzen (*Daily Telegraph*/Kogan Page 1989).

SELLING YOURSELF

Body Langauge, Alan Pease (Sheldon Press, 1988).
CVs and Written Applications, Judy Skeats (Wardlock, 1987).
Effective Networking, Venda Raye-Johnson (Crisp Publications).
Effective Presentation, Anthony Jay (Pitman Publishing 1994).
How to Market Yourself, Ian Phillipson (How To Books 1995)
How to Pass That Interview, Judith Johnstone (How To Books, 1994).
How to Write a CV That Works, Paul McGee (How To Books, 1995).
Presenting Yourself: A Personal Image Guide for Men, Mary Spillane (Piatkus).
Presenting Yourself: A Personal Image Guide for Women, Mary Spillane (Piatkus, 1993).

FUNDING

Department for Education, Publications Centre, PO Box 2193, London E15 2EU. Tel: (0181) 533 2000. Information on grants.
How to Raise Business Finance, Peter Ibbetson (How To Books 1987).
MRC, Project Grants, 20 Park Crescent, London W1N 4AL. Research and training opportunities and project grants.

Further Reading

Sponsorships 1995, COIC, Department CW, ISC05, The Paddock, Frizinghall, Bradford BD9 4HD.
Student Loan Company Ltd, 100 Bothwell Street, Glasgow G2 7GD. Tel: 01345 300 900. Booklet on loans to students.
Tax Relief for Vocational Training, Personal Taxpayers LeafLet IR 119 (Inland Revenue).
The Grant Register (Macmillan Press).

TRAINING AND EDUCATION

British Qualifications, (Kogan Page, 1994). A guide to educational, technical, professional and academic qualifications in Britain.
British Vocation Qualifications, (Kogan Page 1995). A directory of vocational qualifications available from all awarding bodies in Britain.
Degree Course Guides (CRAC, Hobsons Press, bi-annually).
Directory of Further Education, The Comprehensive Guide to Courses in UK Polytechnics and Colleges, James Tomlinson and David Weigall (CRAC, Hobsons Press, annually).
How to Study Effectively, Richard Freeman and John Meed (National Extension College, 1993).
Second Chances: Guide to Adult Education and Training Opportunities, (COIC, 1993).
Unemployment Unit, 409 Brixton Road, London SW9 7DG. Unemployment and training rights handbook.

TIME OUT

The International Directory of Voluntary Work, David Woodworth (Vacation Work, 1989).

POSITIVE THINKING

Creative Visualisation, Sakti Gawain (Bantam 1985).
Effective Thinking Skills, Richard Nelson-Jones (Cassell, 1989).
Feel the Fear and Do It Anyway, Susan Jeffers (Arrow, 1987).
Take Charge of Your Life, Louis Proto (Thorsons, 1988).
Who's Pulling Your Strings, Louis Proto (Thorsons, 1988).

DIRECTORIES

Directory of Directors.

Directory of Grant Making Trusts. List of funds available for research, education and training.

Kelly's Business Directory. Information on over 82,000 industrial, commercial and professional organisations in the UK.

Times 1000 List of Companies. Background information on major companies and establishments offering management and other training courses.

Who Owns Whom. Lists parent companies, their subsidiaries and associates.

BENEFITS

A Guide to Housing Benefit RR2. DSS.
A Guide to Income Support IB20. DSS.
Family Credit Claim Pack FC1. DSS.
Help with the Council Tax CTB1. DSS.
How to Claim State Benefits, Martin Rathfelder (How to Books 1995).
Mortgage Interest Direct IS8. DSS.
One Parent Benefit CH11. DSS.
Self Employed? FB30. DSS.
Unemployed? FB9. DSS.
Unemployment Benefit NI12. DSS.
Voluntary and Part-time Workers FB26. DSS.
Which Benefit? FB2. DSS.

EMPLOYMENT LEGISLATION

Employees's Rights on Insolvency of Employer PL 718. Employment Department.

Facing Redundancy? Time off for Job Hunting or to Arrange Training PL 703. Employment Department.

How to Know Your Rights at Work, Robert Spicer (How To Books, 2nd edition 1995).

Redundancy Consultation and Notification PL 833. Employment Department.

Redundancy Payments PL 808. Employment Department.

Index

Access, 121
Action planning, 141
Adult education, 121
Ageism, 74
Anger, 18
APL, 124
Application forms, 109
Assertiveness, 44

Basic education, 120
Beliefs, 129, 132
Body language, 96
BTEC, 123
Business skills, 89

Career counselling, 12, 64
Career needs and wants, 53
Careers office, 65, 123
CATS, 124
Change, 18, 36, 136
City & Guilds, 123
Communication skills, 96
Confidence building, 80
Contract work, 87, 94
Coping with change, 36
Creating the CV, 75, 103, 106
Criminal record, 77

Dealing with loss, 14

Economic and labour trends, 60
Employment Services, 63
Empowerment, 129
ESOL, 121

Fear, 20
Flexi-time, 87, 94

Floater, 13
Franchises, 86
Funding for courses, 124
Further education, 121
Further reading, 151

Glossary, 142
Goal setting, 136, 139
Government schemes, 122
Grants, 125
Grieving, 17

Healthy eating, 41
Higher education, 122

Image and style, 99
Income, 15
Inner speech, 132
Interim management, 85
Interview techniques, 109

Job competition, 79
Jobcentres, 123
Jobsearch strategy, 62
Jobshare, 87, 94

Lack of experience/skills, 77
Learning skills, 117
Letter writing, 105, 108, 110, 111
Life cycles, 50
Lifestyle, 37
Looking after your health, 38
Loss, 14
Low cost lifestyle, 31

Managing problems, 133
Market research, 89

Material values, 33
Mentor, 13

National Extension College, 122
Networking, 13, 14, 68
Numeracy and literacy, 120
NVQs, 124

Open University, 122
Organising your jobsearch strategy, 60

Part-time work, 87
Personal budgets, 29, 30
Personal fulfilment, 15, 51
Portfolio person, 86, 94
Positive thinking, 23, 34, 42, 133

Raising capital, 89
Reacting to the redundancy, 11
Reading the job advertisement, 101
Redundancy payments, 27
Relaxation techniques, 40
Researching a prospective employer, 65
Returning to study, 62

Saying goodbye, 13
Security zones, 39
Self employment, 88, 94

Self esteem, 15, 21
Self image, 134
Sexism, 74
Skills assessment, 54
Speculative contacts, 66
Sponsor, 14
Stress management, 38
Study skills, 117

TAPS, 65, 122
Telephone skills, 102
Temporary work, 86, 94
Term-time working, 85, 94
The benefit system, 28, 29
The Workers' Educational Association, 121
Thinking skills, 131
Thought processes, 22
Time management, 43
Traditional patterns, 11

Useful addresses, 148
Using the media, 66

Voluntary work, 77

Work values, 12, 51, 82
Working abroad, 88
Working from home, 86, 94

Other Books in this Series

How to Start a New Career
Judith Johnstone

More people than ever before are faced with big career changes today. Few if any jobs are 'for life'. Now in its second edition, this How To book helps you manage your entry into a new career effectively. It is aimed at anyone making a new start, whatever his or her age or background. It looks at who you are and what you are. It helps you evaluate your life skills, to recognise which careers you should concentrate on, and how to make a realistic plan for a happy and productive future. 'Written very much in the style of a work book, with practical exercises and pro formas for the student to complete . . . Well written — would be a useful addition to the library of any guidance practitioner working with adults.' *Newscheck/Careers Service Bulletin.*

140pp illus. 1 85703 139 3. 2nd edition.

How to Start Your Own Business
Jim Green

This dynamic guide fully explores the vital steps to creating a business, interlaced with the author's recent experience in overcoming every hurdle encountered along the way in setting up his own business without capital or discretionary resources. It will show you how to galvanise into initial action, how to source proven ideas, how to write a winning plan, how to approach potential funders, how to present a case for public sector assistance, how to market your business and how to develop the selling habit. No matter what your age or personal circumstances, you *can* strike out on your own, create an enterprise and change your life for the better. Jim Green is chairman and managing director of Focus Publishing International Ltd and for many years specialised in founding, buying and selling advertising agencies.

160pp illus. 1 85703 122 9.

How to Work From Home
Ian Phillipson

Working from home is no longer a cottage industry. Improved technology, computers and faxes now allow professional, creative and business people of every kind to switch away from the traditional workplace and still communicate effectively with colleagues, suppliers and customers. This popular title in the **How To** series provides a complete step-by-step guide to successful planning and organisation of what is fast becoming the preferred option for millions of individuals in the new work environment of the 1990s. 'A wonderful book written by a man with a splendid sense of humour and a good practical approach. It concentrates on the key techniques that will make you really efficient yet comfortable when working from home, and able to compete on equal terms with even the most efficient firms and organisations.' *Home Run Magazine.*

176 pp illus. 1 85703 158 X. 2nd edition.

How to Start a Business From Home
Graham Jones

Most people have dreamed of starting their own business from home at some time or other, but how do you begin? The third edition of this popular book contains a wealth of ideas, projects, tips, facts, checklists and quick-reference information for everyone — whether in between jobs, taking early retirement, or students and others with time to invest. Packed with information on everything from choosing a good business idea and starting up to advertising, book-keeping and dealing with professionals, this book is basic reading for every budding entrepreneur. 'Full of ideas and advice.' *The Daily Mirror.* 'This book is essential — full of practical advice.' *Home Run.* Graham Jones BSc(Hons) is an editor, journalist and lecturer specialising in practical business subjects. His other books include *Fit to Manage* and *The Business of Freelancing.*

176 pp illus. 1 85703 126 1. 3rd edition.

How to Raise Business Finance
Peter Ibbetson

'Gives the right amount of information.' *Association of British Chambers of Commerce.* 'A lucid account of the steps by which a small businessman can substantially strengthen his case.' *The Financial Times.* Peter Ibbetson is an Associate of the Chartered Institute of Bankers, and an author and broadcaster on banking matters.

160pp illus. 07463 0338 6.

How to Apply for a Job
Judith Johnstone

Tough new realities are dominating the jobs market. It is no longer enough to send employers lists of worthy past achievements or vague details of hobbies and 'interests'. Employers want to know: 'What skills can you offer? What can you do for us, and how fast? What personal commitment will you put on the line? What value for money will you be? Whether you are short term or long term unemployed, a school or college leaver, or mature returner to the workplace, this book shows you how to clarify what you can really offer, and how to market this effectively to meet an employment need. 'Very practical and informative.' *Phoenix/Association of Graduate Careers Advisory Services.*

160pp illus. 1 85703 138 5. 2nd edition.

How to Claim State Benefits
Martin Rathfelder

The Welfare State changes all the time. The third edition of this book has been completely rewritten to take full account of the abolition of the poll tax, mobility allowance, invalidity benefit and unemployment benefit, and the introduction of council tax, disability living allowance, incapacity benefit and jobseeker's allowance — as well as many minor changes. It is the only popular paperback which explains the whole range of benefits available from local and central government, showing you exactly how to claim, and how to arrange your affairs to take advantage of the current benefit system.

160pp illus. 1 85703 073 7. 3rd edition.

How to Pass That Interview
Judith Johnstone

Everyone knows how to shine at interview — or do they? When every candidate becomes the perfect clone of the one before, you have to have that extra 'something' to raise your chances above the rest. Using a systematic and practical approach, this **How To** book takes you step-by-step through the essential pre-interview groundwork, the interview encounter itself, and what you can learn from the experience afterwards. The book contains sample pre- and post-interview correspondence, and is complete with a guide to further reading, glossary of terms, and index. 'This is from the first class How To Books stable.' *Escape Committee Newsletter.* 'Offers a fresh approach to a well documented subject.' *Newscheck/Careers Service Bulletin.* 'A complete step-by-step guide.' *The Association of Business Executives.* Judith Johnstone is a Graduate of the Institute of Personnel & Development; she has been an instructor in Business Studies and adult literacy tutor, and has long experience of helping people at work.

128pp illus. 1 85703 118 0. 2nd edition.

Other Books in this Series

How to Get That Job
Joan Fletcher

Now in its third edition this popular book provides a clear step-by-step guide to identifying job opportunities, writing successful application letters, preparing for interviews and being selected. 'A valuable book.' *Teachers Weekly*. 'Cheerful and appropriate . . . particularly helpful in providing checklists designed to bring system to searching for a job. This relaxed, friendly and very helpful little book could bring lasting benefit.' *Times Educational Supplement*. 'Clear and concise . . . should be mandatory reading by all trainees.' *Comlon Magazine (LCCI)*. Joan Fletcher is an experienced Manager and Student Counsellor.

112pp illus. 1 85703 096 6. 3rd edition.

How to Market Yourself
Ian Phillipson

In today's intensely competitive workplace it has become ever more vital to market yourself effectively, whether as a first-time job hunter, existing employee, or mature returner. This hard-hitting new manual provides a really positive step-by-step guide to assessing yourself, choosing the right personal image, identifying and presenting the right skills, building confidence, marketing yourself in person and on paper, organising your self-marketing campaign, using mentors at work, selling yourself to colleagues, clients and customers, and marketing yourself for a fast-changing future. The book is complete with checklists, assignments and case studies.

160pp illus. 1 85703 160 1.

How to Write a CV That Works
Paul McGee

What makes a CV stand out from the crowd? How can you present yourself in the most successful way? This practical book shows you how to develop different versions of your CV for every situation. Reveal your hidden skills, identify your achievements and learn how to communicate these successfully. Different styles and uses for a CV are examined, as you discover the true importance of your most powerful marketing tool. Paul McGee is a freelance Trainer and Consultant for one of Britain's largest outplacement organisations. He conducts Marketing Workshops for people from all walks of life.

128pp illus. 1 85703 171 7.